Fort Bragg to Hué

Fort Bragg to Hué

*A Paratrooper with the 82nd
and 173rd Airborne in Vietnam,
1968–1970*

JAMES M. DORN

Major, USAR (Ret.)

McFarland & Company, Inc., Publishers

Jefferson, North Carolina

LIBRARY OF CONGRESS CATALOGUING-IN-PUBLICATION DATA

Names: Dorn, James M., 1945– author.
Title: Fort Bragg to Hué : a paratrooper with the 82nd and 173rd Airborne
in Vietnam, 1968–1970 / James M. Dorn, Maj IN, USAR (Ret.).
Description: Jefferson, North Carolina : McFarland & Company, Inc.,
Publishers, 2023 | Includes index.
Identifiers: LCCN 2022039442 | ISBN 9781476689333 (paperback : acid free paper) ∞
ISBN 9781476646732 (ebook)
Subjects: LCSH: Dorn, James M., 1945– | United States. Army—Officers—
Biography. | United States. Army—Parachute troops—Biography. | United States.
Army. Airborne Division, 82nd. Brigade, 3rd—History—20th century. | United
States. Army. Airborne Brigade, 173rd—History—20th century. | Vietnam War,
1961–1975—Personal narratives, American. | BISAC: HISTORY /
Wars & Conflicts / Vietnam War
Classification: LCC DS558.4 .D67 2023 | DDC 959.704/3092 [B]—dc23/eng/20220920
LC record available at https://lccn.loc.gov/2022039442

BRITISH LIBRARY CATALOGUING DATA ARE AVAILABLE

ISBN (print) 978-1-4766-8933-3
ISBN (ebook) 978-1-4766-4673-2

Front cover image: Captain James Dorn in dress uniform,
early 1970s; the Combat Service Identification Badge
or the 82nd Airborne Division; the Combat Service Identification Badge
for the 173rd Airborne Brigade (all images author collection);
background © Robin Kay/Shutterstock

Printed in the United States of America

*McFarland & Company, Inc., Publishers
Box 611, Jefferson, North Carolina 28640
www.mcfarlandpub.com*

Table of Contents

Table of Contents

Dedicated to the paratroopers of the 3rd Brigade, 82nd Airborne Division and the 173rd Airborne Brigade with whom I was privileged to serve during the two consecutive years I spent in Vietnam. We went side by side on our never-ending marches to engage the North Vietnamese Army and the Viet Cong. This is the greatest honor of my life.

Acknowledgments

My love and thanks go to Jo Anna, my wife, and Michael, my son, for putting up with my telling and retelling the stories of my adventures and misadventures in Vietnam, and for supporting me as I wrote this, and for the occasional hug.

In Memoriam

Donald W. Dorn, Captain, USMC, my father, was a career officer, ground attack pilot, and an instructor pilot in the United States Marine Corps during World War II and the Korean War. He was killed in action while attacking an enemy truck convoy in North Korea. He flew with VMF(N) 513, the Flying Nightmares. *Semper Fi, Gentlemen*. I have missed his presence all my life since.

Donald M. Dorn, my young brother, was another victim of the Chinese Virus. I miss him. He served on the USS *Ranger*, an aircraft carrier off the coast of the Republic of Vietnam.

Dori Ellen Hankins, my beautiful sister and youngest sibling, who, for reasons known only to God, loved her oldest brother. I miss her very much too.

An Infantryman's Lot

By the Author

I have carried my equipment and arms for miles,
Through jungle, swamp, rice paddy and desert,
Over beach, rivers, mountains, and snow.
My pack straps, they dig into my shoulders,
And the pain is a constant throbbing.
My shirt is often soaked with sweat,
Hot by day and cold by night.
I have slept when I could, often cold,
Wet or near frozen, but never deeply.
I have gone without food or water for days.
I have bled from wounds, small and grievous.
I have seen Death come nigh to my comrades,
To take away their pain and suffering
And leave in their place, the peace of the grave.
I stand between the foe, my countrymen, and my nation.
I shall not halt nor slacken my pace,
Nor falter or fail, for the enemy is at hand.
Here, I shall stand and, if need be, fall.
For I am an American Soldier.

Preface

I wrote this memoir for five reasons. First: In my research, I couldn't find a single book describing the activities of the 3rd Brigade, 82nd Airborne Division in Vietnam. It was as if the roughly four thousand paratroopers—who deployed there as reinforcements in the battles to counter the enemy's Tet Offensive of 1968 and who fought valiantly in the battles to crush the North Vietnamese Army (NVA) around Hué in the I Corps zone or later when we protected Saigon in III Corps—never fought there. I've tried to fill in some of the gaps.

Second: I document the many places I saw, the things I experienced, and the events my men and I experienced in my two years in Vietnam. I served in three of the four military zones into which the Republic of Vietnam was divided, north to south. I Corps with Hué and the Demilitarized Zone was in the North, II and III Corps with Saigon occupied the middle of the country, and IV Corps was the southernmost.

Third: I also describe the activities of the 173rd Airborne Brigade to which I transferred for my second year in Vietnam. I once again led Infantry platoons of paratroopers, but this time in combat operations in the Central Highlands where our enemy was the North Vietnamese Army and later the Viet Cong (VC) in the coastal lowlands in II Corps

Fourth: Most of the existing nonfiction works focus on specific battles. I recount fourteen months of the daily activities of the three Infantry platoons I led in combat operations at different times. I also describe another eleven months where I served as a new second lieutenant and staff officer in the headquarters of the 3rd Brigade, and as a new captain and assistant operations staff officer in the 173rd Air-borne Brigade's 3rd Battalion, 503rd Parachute Infantry Regiment.

Fifth: This is my unabashed try for immortality.

Everything I wrote here, good or bad, is the absolute truth. The opinions are mine.

PART ONE

The 3rd Brigade, 82nd Airborne Division

The Combat Service Identification Badge for the 82nd Airborne Division

1

From Emergency Alert to Arrival in Vietnam

12 February 1968 to 14 February 1968

I arrived in the Republic of Vietnam on Valentine's Day 1968. Who says the U.S. Army doesn't have a sense of humor? However, I wasn't alone; the lead units of the 3rd Brigade of the 82nd Airborne Division arrived with me. Ultimately, nearly four thousand paratroopers with their weapons and vehicles would join us. What had happened? The NVA and VC's Tet Offensive.

Please bear with me. A little of my history before that date is necessary. My part of this story began less than three months before I arrived in Vietnam. I received my commission as a second lieutenant in the Army Infantry on November 19, 1967. Three weeks later, the colonel commanding the Army's Airborne School pinned my Parachutist's Badge onto my chest on the drop zone after the last of our five training jumps.

It was a proud moment for me. I now enjoyed the elite status of a paratrooper. My orders assigned me to one of the Army's elite combat units, the 82nd Airborne Infantry Division. A joke says the men get separated from the boys in the first week of Jump School. The men get separated from the idiots during the second week. The idiots jump out of airplanes in flight during the third or jump week. If you complete all five jumps you become a parachutist, a soldier entitled to wear the Parachutist's Badge on your uniform.

I enjoyed parachuting. I had managed to make a half dozen or so parachute jumps in the first thirty days after I arrived at the

2

division. I didn't make another parachute jump for more than two years.

The 82nd is a Light Infantry unit. It didn't have the larger artillery, armored vehicles and numbers of trucks the regular Infantry divisions possessed. It did have a tradition of valorous service in war dating back to World War I. Sergeant Alvin York of World War I fame earned the Medal of Honor for his actions in combat while serving in the 82nd Airborne Division. The men of the division in World War II served with great distinction in a number of major battles.

More importantly, the 82nd possessed the capability of rapid deployment by air. The Department of the Army designated the 82nd as its Rapid Reaction Force for this reason. The Joint Chiefs of Staff randomly tested the division's ability to immediately deploy one fully manned brigade to wherever the Pentagon wanted. Each was a timed exercise with short response times.

It usually meant nothing more than having the designated brigade, everyone equipped with his load-bearing equipment, his M-16 rifle and a parachute, to report to the marshaling yards by a specified time. All of our heavy equipment and heavier weapons, pre-rigged for a parachute drop or air landing, awaited the designated brigade there.

Sometimes it meant getting everyone there by a specified time. Others required boarding aircraft, flying around for a while, and then executing a mass parachute drop on one of Fort Bragg's Drop Zones to complete the exercise. Occasionally, the brigade would parachute into a location far from Ft. Bragg.

I, a freshly minted U.S. Army Infantry second lieutenant and paratrooper, was assigned to the 82nd Airborne Division, "The All Americans," with a reporting date of January 4, 1968. Ultimately, I was assigned to A Company, 2nd Battalion, 505th Parachute Infantry Regiment (PIR) of the 3rd Brigade—505th Parachute Infantry Regiment, 3rd Brigade, 82nd Airborne Division, to give its complete name. Thank God for abbreviations.

Forty-four infantrymen counting its officer make up the strength of a standard Infantry platoon. This one boasted of only two paratroopers, the platoon sergeant and me. This did give me the benefit of rapid roll calls.

The company commanding officer (CO), another but less recently minted second lieutenant tasked me with helping prepare for one of the Army's intensive administrative inspections of its units. Failing this inspection could end the commander's career.

February 12, 1968, a Monday, began in the usual fashion of the Army. My CO returned from a morning briefing at battalion headquarters. He brought the answer to the single question on every second lieutenant's mind. "When will I receive orders to Vietnam?" He told us to expect our orders one year from the date we received our commissions. I would receive my orders in late November. I breathed a metaphysical sigh of relief as a great weight lifted from my shoulders. I had time to learn my job as a rifle or Infantry platoon leader before leading men in combat. If I was given troops to lead.

My relief died within a handful of hours. The battalion commander called all the company commanders to another briefing in the afternoon. When our CO returned, he told our first sergeant to lock all of the barrack doors and ordered that "no one enters or leaves." I thought it sounded like the Pentagon ordered us to execute another test emergency deployment. I lacked the relevant experience to know better.

Not long after my CO returned with the alert news, he sent me to battalion headquarters to pick up the platoon leaders of the rifle platoons which would bring "A" Company to full strength. I arrived in time to catch the end of their briefing. "You will pick up jungle fatigues and boots in-country." Some words stay with you for a lifetime. These have. There anticipation of finding out our destination vanished, replaced with a degree of surprise.

I knew the Army only equipped its troops with jungle fatigues and jungle boots in two locations in early 1968. The Jungle Training School in Panama was one. For the Joint Chiefs of Staff to allow its entire Army Rapid Reaction Force to undergo jungle training in Panama at one time was inconceivable. Extricating them, returning them to Ft. Bragg, and refitting them for a real emergency deployment involved too much time.

1. From Emergency Alert to Arrival in Vietnam

The other place where wearing jungle fatigues and jungle boots was the norm was the Republic of South Vietnam. Like Sherlock Holmes, I deduced our destination. Our alert was no longer a routine exercise. The 3rd Brigade's orders sent it into another war, sucking me right along in the vacuum left by its passage.

We now-excess second lieutenants found ourselves in a predicament. We'd been replaced and were no longer platoon leaders. We'd technically become homeless.

Those emergency deployment orders from the Joint Chiefs of Staff sent nearly four thousand paratroopers in three Infantry battalions and one Artillery battalion, plus trucks and helicopters, into the final preparations to board the many U.S. Air Force C-141 jet transports waiting at Pope Air Force Base to fly us to Vietnam. We and some Marines were the reinforcements for the hard-pressed United States and Vietnamese forces battling North Vietnamese regiments in the area in and around the old city of Hué.

Despite being at only 35 percent of its authorized strength, the 82nd Airborne Division remained the U.S. Army's Rapid Reaction Force. The three Infantry brigades divided the available men between them. A more accurate term is they created three shell (empty) brigades, meaning each of the Infantry companies consisted of one full strength platoon and two empty ones.

But we were a fighting force of mostly battle-hardened paratroopers. They'd experienced combat in at least one tour in Vietnam. This time the 3rd Brigade took nearly everybody in the division. I heard the division's area looked like a ghost town after we departed.

If a paratrooper returned from Vietnam yesterday, we took him with us. If a paratrooper's release from active duty date came in more than thirty days, we took him. I never imagined the volume of inquiries the division received from parents, wives, or girlfriends about the well-being of specific paratroopers. The division forwarded them to us for action after we arrived in Vietnam.

The division's capability to deploy a full-strength brigade involved transferring the full-strength Infantry platoons of two of the shell Infantry brigades to bring the deploying brigade up to full strength. The Pentagon's plans took our lack of men into account.

Part One—The 3rd Brigade, 82nd Airborne Division

They tasked the division to be ready to deploy one fully-manned brigade to anywhere in the world on one- or two-days' notice.

The Tet Offensive began two weeks earlier during the night of January 30. The heavy and successful attacks by the North Vietnamese Army (NVA) and the Viet Cong (VC) on major cities throughout South Vietnam caused General William Westmoreland, the commander of the Military Assistance Command, Vietnam (MACV), to call for reinforcements to help defeat the enemy forces in those attacks. He specifically requested an airborne brigade and a regiment of U.S. Marines. He got us, the 3rd Brigade of the 82nd Airborne Infantry Division. We were the last of the U.S. Army's Rapid Reaction Force.

President Lyndon Johnson set our deployment in motion on February 12, 1968, when he gave the command to send reinforcements to Vietnam. *Et voila*, the 3rd Brigade stood ready for combat. Due to the division's many rehearsals for rapid deployment, this one worked beautifully, except for one small problem. The 3rd Brigade's three-month period in the rotation as the deploying brigade ended January 31. The honor belonged to another brigade.

Practical considerations outweighed the technicality of our turn having ended. The 3rd Brigade's vehicles, artillery, helicopters and large pieces of equipment sat at the marshaling yards at nearby Pope Air Base all pre-rigged for air, land or airdrop missions. The current alert brigade was still getting their equipment ready. These facts tipped the balance in the 3rd Brigade's favor. On such small things hang the major turning points in our lives.

I anticipated receiving orders to Vietnam someday. For an Infantry officer it went without saying. But I never considered the possibility it would happen in this manner. I needed more time to gain proficiency in the practical aspects of commanding a rifle platoon. However, the fickle finger of fate chose February 12, 1968, to intervene. It dictated I'd learn my craft in the crucible of a shooting war.

South Vietnam's chief weather feature is nationwide humidity. Although unpleasant for most of the year, the humidity brings misery in the hot dry season. The one exception, the Central Highlands, has weather which is less humid, and stays cooler in the dry season. This played a role in another fateful decision many months later.

The monsoon season brings near constant rains or drizzle from low-lying clouds. In the higher elevations, the clouds blanket the mountaintops and reach down to the surrounding hilltops, adding to the large amount of moisture from the rains, thus making up for the reduction in humidity.

The possibility of actually going into battle gave me reason to inwardly pause. I did not fear the idea of engaging in combat. I feared getting my men needlessly killed or wounded. I worried about my reaction to people shooting at me. I wouldn't know how I would react until the first time I came under enemy fire. It preys on you; it really does. Not constantly but it pops up at the strangest times.

Thankfully, when the time came, I reacted instantly and correctly. I shot back. Curiously, I was angry about coming under small arms fire, but not concerned. I knew my character traits did not include cowardice.

This is important to me. Three consecutive generations of the men of my family served in the United States Armed Forces in times of war. Each of us took the oath "to support and defend the Constitution of the United States against all enemies, foreign or domestic and bear true faith and allegiance to the same." I did not want to be the first to run or break my oath.

Each of us received orders to bring our military fatigues and equipment plus our civilian clothes. I obtained permission to return to my off-post residence to pick up my military gear along with whatever else they told us to bring. I'm still mystified why we brought all of it with us. I never saw most of it again. I followed orders. Like all the rest, I stuffed everything into two duffel bags.

I told my roommate, a former OCS classmate, about the situation. I asked him to take care of the rest of my things, including my new car, until someone from my family came to take them home for me. He remained with the 82nd Airborne Division at Ft. Bragg. I never saw him again.

I took a few minutes to call my uncle Jim Curtis in California. He was a former U.S. Marine who lived not far from my family. I asked him to collect my things because my unit received orders for an emergency deployment. I said nothing about our destination. He knew the only emergency receiving constant play in the media remained the heavy fighting in Vietnam since Tet. I asked him to break the news to my mother, a Korean War widow.

Later, I learned he brought my maternal grandmother with him. They drove my car back to California. I'm told they enjoyed the trip. I drove a similar route in December 1967. I heartily recommend a cross-country drive through America if you want to see it up close.

The delivery of the news of my going to a combat zone required certain sensitivity. A Japanese soldier on Okinawa in World War II killed my father's younger brother Lance Corporal Darwin Dorn, USMC. My mother liked him and mourned his loss. My father, 1st Lt. Donald Walker Dorn, USMC, a career Marine and highly respected ground attack instructor pilot, served during World War II. He finally got his chance to serve in combat in the Korean War.

The North Koreans shot him down one night in October 1951. He was attacking a North Korean convoy at night. The crash site and his remains have never been located. My mother loved him beyond measure. I am their first-born. She told me she loved all of their sons but I was special in her eyes.

The Marine Corps declared my father dead after two years. I vaguely remember how my mother reacted, but I know she took it hard. Words like inconsolable or devastated come to mind. In February 1968, I worried how she'd receive my deployment to Vietnam. I figured not well.

The night of the 12th, every member of the company, including the superfluous second lieutenants, received a brand-new M-16A1 rifle to replace our existing used ones. We stayed busy getting ready throughout the long night. To keep occupied, I rigged the sling on the new M-16A1 to suit me. Otherwise, I helped as needed. The following morning, February 13, 1968, we got orders to "Saddle Up," meaning grab all our gear and weapons and then head out to the trucks waiting to take us to nearby Pope Air Force Base.

1. From Emergency Alert to Arrival in Vietnam

This phase took place without event although the soldiers tasked to drive our duffel bags to the airfield displayed a minor bit of truculence. A two-and-a-half-ton rated truck, complete with a driver plus his assistant, stopped in our company's barracks. The truculence came from the driver.

Picture the scene. Each paratrooper carried an M-16. He wore a steel helmet, a load-bearing harness with a filled canteen, and his backpack containing his field equipment. He also carried two large duffel bags by their handles or on his shoulders. The total weight is considerable and awkward to handle. It takes luck merely to lift the duffel bags one by one onto the tailgate. The driver or his assistant expected these paratroopers to climb onto the truck and stack the bags at the front end of the truck bed.

The paratroopers stood in a long line. Each waited his turn to toss his duffel bags onto the truck's tailgate, climb up to the truck bed to reposition the bags, and climb down, all while trying to not drop anything. A long time does not begin to describe the probable delay of our departure for Pope AFB.

I asked the driver and his assistant to lift the duffel bags from the tailgate and stack them further back in the truck's bed. They refused, saying their job did not include stacking the bags. I took one look at them followed by a look at the line of paratroopers weighed down with their gear but ready to obey their orders. I gave the driver and his assistant a direct order to get into the bed of the truck and stack the duffel bags when they landed on the tailgate. The driver responded with a threat to report me to their commanding officer (CO). His threat paled into insignificance compared to the threats awaiting me in Vietnam.

I told them I didn't care what they did but my direct order gave them one option: obey it immediately. I wanted these paratroopers to get the assistance they needed with loading their duffel bags. The two obeyed my order. They helped load and stack the men's duffel bags. Offloading at Pope AFB went well. When I look back, I believe this minor dust-up foretold a part of my future.

A Long, Uncomfortable, Boring Flight to Vietnam in a C-141

Seeing the United States was interesting as we crossed the nation but only if you had a window. Crossing the Pacific Ocean is the very definition of boring. After watching the first dozen miles of ocean pass under us, all interest in the next five and a half thousand miles faded away. Sadly, I had not thought to bring any books to read on the flight. Every flight I made to or from Vietnam from the United States was boring. The only remedy was sleep.

Sleeping on a C-141 did not come easy. The C-141 had been fitted with "seats" for troop transport, which demonstrates its versatility. We couldn't stand or sit on the floor of the cargo area. The four rows of seats ran lengthwise in the aircraft with the two outboard rows facing inward and the two inboard rows sitting back-to-back down the centerline facing outwards. Our duffel bags lay in an inviting large mound on the tail ramp. The cargo master forbade this.

The backs and seats consisted of sheets of red nylon stretched tight over tubular aluminum frames. We sat upright because the seats did not recline. I thought we bore a strong resemblance to canned sardines. Anyone sitting packed in those minimal seats long enough will want to jump out of the plane with or without a parachute!

Each aircraft contained a "comfort package." I came to realize "comfort" is a misnomer. Its use belied a perverse desire of the designer to further torment us. "Comfort package" means restrooms, a tiny kitchen to serve one hundred forty or so young men a frozen dinner, plus storage for box lunches. The restrooms only remained clean for the first few hours. The word disgusting comes to mind but does not adequately describe the later level of disgust.

The kitchen provided a microwave oven to heat up frozen dinners for all on board. It also provided refrigeration to keep perishables and drinks cold. However, today's civilian flights, despite the loss of the free amenities, provide better service, i.e., small bags of pretzels!

The pilot of our C-141 invited the officers to visit the flight deck one at a time to look around. The visibility through the cockpit windows afforded a fantastic view for miles in any direction of clear weather, blue skies, scattered white clouds, and an empty Pacific Ocean five or six miles below. I thought it excellent flying weather. Years later, I learned about the threat of clear air turbulence.

The flight deck of a C-141 is spacious, not cramped like the ones on commercial airliners. It looked like a comfortable place to work. The long-haul commercial airliners had a couple of sleeping compartments to allow the pilots to rest in rotation. I saw a long, well-padded bench seat along the back wall of the cockpit. The idea of a nap on that comfy seat came unbidden to my mind. One of the officers told me the flight crews took naps on it during long flights like ours. We paratroopers sat in the extra cheap seats in the cargo section.

Our first refueling stop came at Elmendorf Air Force Base outside Anchorage, Alaska. February is a cold, snow-filled month in Anchorage. We deplaned down rollout stairs to the tarmac. We walked in the freezing cold to the terminal to wait to reboard. While we waited, the ground crew refueled the C-141. With the refueling done, the ground crew replaced the original comfort package with a new one for the next never-ending leg.

The Air Force gave us the unpleasant news that officers must pay for their rations for the remainder of the flight. This caused some consternation among the officers. The Army placed us on paid rations status in our orders to deploy to Vietnam. It seems the Air Force did not know this or care. One of us stood on principle. He refused to pay the roughly three dollars per meal or about eleven dollars for the remainder of the flight. The Air Force Cargo Master did not provide him with any food, although he did get water. Those who, like me, preferred eating to hunger paid for the meals. We did not let him go hungry and shared our meals with him.

Hunger trumped principle despite the meal's lack of taste. The main course in one frozen meal masqueraded as a tough, tasteless steak. Our box lunches consisted of dry cheese sandwiches, small packages of various chips, a small can of fruit juice, and a piece of fruit. All I can say is they kept us from starving.

Looking out a window to watch endless miles of featureless ocean passing below has no entertainment value. I tried to sleep to no avail. Nothing changed, except the temperature dropped. Otherwise, we slept fitfully, if at all. Meanwhile the C-141 droned nearer to Vietnam.

We arrived over Vietnam before dawn. The sleepy faces of men curious to see something of their destination filled the windows. We knew Vietnam lay below us but we did not know any specific place name. Learning our exact destination would have to wait until our C-141 landed in Vietnam. Finally, the pilot gave us a cheery "Welcome to Chu Lai, Vietnam" over the public address system. I knew virtually nothing about the map of Vietnam. Consequently, Chu Lai meant nothing to me.

I felt a sense of expectancy, not fear mind you, from all of the paratroopers. It felt like what a runner experiences immediately before the starting pistol is fired. It could also have been nothing more than the eagerness to get out of a cramped and uncomfortable aircraft at last. Curiously, I think each of us feels something similar in the minute after we hear the "One Minute" warning before jumping from an aircraft to parachute down to Earth.

Our lead unit, along with me, landed at Chu Lai Air Base about two hours before dawn on Valentine's Day. Unfamiliar odors of strange places coupled with those of rotting vegetation assaulted my sense of smell as I walked down the C-141's tail cargo ramp into the dank gloom of the taxiway. Clearly the C-141 did not land us in Kansas. Over time, I ceased to notice the odors. However, I noticed the humidity nearly every hour of every day.

A light drizzle, little more than a mist, greeted me. Low, thick cloud formations over the air base completely obscured all light from the night sky. The few lights on the ground, plus the runway lights and the light from the C-141's interior, provided what illumination there was. There was little to see.

The cool, damp night air made our arrival more unpleasant. Worse, the fine-grained sand alongside the taxiway clung to our boots, uniforms, and anything else it touched. I tried to dust it off of my fatigues only to end up with most of it on my hands.

The arrival of dawn brought more proof I did indeed stand on foreign soil. Everyone, save us, wore jungle fatigues. This ruled out any chance of me merely dreaming in my bed in my apartment outside Fort Bragg.

My thoughts turned briefly to the great change in my future by the VC and the NVA brought about by their Vietnam-wide Tet Offensive. However, getting our gear, M-16s and ammunition off of the C-141 took precedence over what the future held.

An Air Force ground crewman, curious about seeing one hundred forty-odd, armed and combat equipped Army infantrymen, asked who we were. His was a good question given our deployment bore a much-violated classification of "secret." One of us answered, "We're the 82nd Airborne." The crewman looked unimpressed with this answer.

He asked something like, "What are you doing here?" in his follow-up question.

This was an unexpected question. The way the media portrayed the enemy's Tet Offensive made some of us, me included, expect to step out of the C-141 and straight into battle. One of us told him we're here to save you.

The crewman said, "Really?" in a questioning tone.

We expected a more enthusiastic reception because of the media's horrific descriptions of the fierce battles of the Tet Offensive. His attitude brought some disappointment to our arrival. Horrific battles were happening in major cities, but it seemed they did not occur everywhere.

15 February 1968 to 1 March 1968

My comrades of a few weeks and I lost our official positions with the brigade once we landed. This happened because the filler platoons came with first or second lieutenants. This presented no problem at first. We all underwent a mildly interesting one-week course to familiarize us with Viet Cong ambush tactics and booby traps. The American Division, aka the 23rd Infantry Division, put it on. I believe General Colin Powell served as a captain with the American during his second tour in Vietnam in 1968. I didn't encounter him.

I experienced one of the moments that give one pause. Around lunchtime, the enemy fired a 122mm (roughly four inches in diameter by six feet long) rocket into the base. This single rocket attack displayed some odd features. One, it took place in daytime when most rocket attacks occurred at night. Two, the enemy fired only one rocket. The riveting part occurred after it hit one of the Air Force's bomb storage facilities.

The facility exploded more than a mile distant from me. The explosion remains one of the three loudest sounds in my life. It shook the ground for a few seconds. The concussion struck with only a mild force due to the great distance it traveled. I saw my first real-life mushroom cloud. It reached a few thousand feet into the air. That mushroom cloud ended any remaining doubt that I stood in a war zone. The picture lies etched into my memory. I carry many such memories, some good and some bad.

About this time, the news media displayed photographs of President Lyndon Johnson bidding farewell to the 1st Battalion of the 505th, calling it the lead unit of the reinforcements going to Vietnam. To correct the historical record, the 2nd Battalion of the 505th and I arrived in Vietnam several days prior to when the 1st Battalion left Ft. Bragg. President Johnson possessed the politician's desire for media coverage. We all know politicians continue to bend the truth to their needs.

After the familiarization course, the 2nd Battalion began a few days of low-level combat operations around Chu Lai to get the kinks out. This is necessary before facing the possibility of a large-scale battle. We found a glitch developed in the plan; we lacked fragmentation grenades and colored smoke grenades to use in close combat.

When calling in an air strike you need to ensure the bombs or rockets fall only on the enemy. Those colored smoke grenades help to avoid tragic mistakes but nothing in war comes with a guarantee.

Important point: always ask what ordnance the fixed wing aircraft carries. The variations in ordnance make a big, perhaps lifesaving, difference if you know the ordnance being dropped. If you call for a close-in air support, make napalm your last resort.

We managed to get our hands on some variously colored smoke grenades. We excess second lieutenants handed them out to our units exiting through Chu Lai's perimeter defenses. We could not get our hands on fragmentation grenades. Luckily, the men of the 2nd Battalion did not contact the enemy.

The 2nd Battalion went north by truck convoy to join the fighting around Hué. They traveled north about 99 kilometers (61.5 miles) to Da Nang. They stayed overnight there to avoid the risk of an enemy ambush in the notorious Hai Van Pass immediately north of Da Nang. My understanding is nearly everyone in Da Nang sort of cheered to see the 2nd Battalion when they arrived. Little cheering accompanied the 2nd Battalion's departure the next morning. It seems a large number of items disappeared while they stayed overnight.

As I said earlier, airborne units are light infantry. They lack the same amount or variety of equipment the regular and mechanized infantry units enjoy. It seems the combat veterans of the 2nd Battalion tried to liberate a lot of things to make up for the equipment deficiencies during their overnight stay in Da Nang.

The 2nd Battalion's convoy continued north for another 82 kilometers (51 miles) to its new home on a huge base 12 kilometers (8 miles) south of Hué. It bore the name Gia Le Combat Base. We called it Phu Bai after the nearby village. The Marines operated a small airfield there. In addition to the 3rd Brigade, it held the rear echelons of U.S. Marines, U.S. Navy Construction Battalion (Seabees) and the 101st Airborne Division (Screaming Eagles). The 3rd Brigade fell under the operational control (OPCON) of the 101st.

The 1st Battalion arrived in Da Nang something like two weeks later. It did not receive a warm welcome. Instead, the Military Police (MPs) met it at the southern gate. They escorted the convoy to a barbed wire enclosure for the duration of their overnight stay. The MPs guarded it there to make sure no more thefts occurred. They escorted the 1st Battalion out of Da Nang the following morning.

I suppose I ought to show some outrage about the 2nd Battalion's conduct, but I don't. The life of a paratrooper in combat depends partly on making the most of what he brings with him or his capability to supplement what he brought with him. His survival in battle depends on him taking liberties with the execution of his orders when necessary. These qualities encourage the independent thinking behind the actions underlying the American paratrooper's reputation for fierceness in battle, especially in defensive operations.

The classification "Light Infantry" in no way means United States paratroopers are pushovers. The Germans learned this truth on D-Day, in Belgium during Operation Market-Garden, and at Bastogne during the Battle of the Bulge.

These men knew what awaited them around Hué. They "liberated" the things which offered the opportunity to make their lives a bit less primitive between battles. They fought well, they fought by the rules, they won and they survived. No other measure of a combat unit's effectiveness counts.

A short time later I received orders to join the brigade's headquarters south of Hué. Units of the brigade had engaged the enemy around Hué not long after arriving at Gia Le Combat Base.

2

The Brigade's Public Information Staff Officer

2 March 1968 to 26 August 1968

Staff Life in Gia Le Combat Base

My orders to join brigade headquarters took me to Gia Le Combat Base. The United States Marine Corps controlled the base, which covered enough land to allow construction of the Marines administrative headquarters, supply support, and rear echelons of the Marine units in the Hué area and north to the Demilitarized Zone (DMZ).

I flew to Phu Bai in a C-47 transport aircraft. I think it was manufactured near the time I was born. It earned a place in history when it dropped paratroopers from the 82nd and 101st Airborne Divisions into Normandy in the hours of darkness preceding the D-Day landings on the beaches of Normandy.

This slow aircraft had a top speed of about 224 mph but cruised about 160 mph. A couple of slightly open windows provided a pleasant airflow in the cabin. Its comfort level exceeds most modern jet airliners. I had a terrific flight.

The 3rd Brigade Headquarters was identified by a large sign. Its staff sections, the headquarters of the various battalions, other units, and barracks were nearby. I saw the area was festooned with antennae guide wires, tent tie down ropes and the steel stakes to fix them in place.

A few excess second lieutenants, like myself, received temporary

3rd Brigade Headquarters, 82nd Airborne Division sign in Gia Le Combat Base, 12 kilometers south of Hué 1968.

assignments to the brigade's S-1 (Personnel Administration Staff Section) to handle the tsunami of inquiries from families about their paratroopers. We also received a few inquiries from some members of Congress. This required special handling above the pay grade of a second lieutenant.

We handled dozens of inquiries every day for more than two weeks. Our abrupt semi-secret departure from Ft. Bragg caused this problem. To make matters worse it took time to establish our mail service through the Army's mail system in Vietnam.

We telephoned our counterparts in the battalion S-1s and other units assigned to the brigade. Brigade S-1 kept track of casualty information. Consequently, we only needed to ask if the soldier in question was healthy. Next, we requested the folks in the battalion S-1s to tell the individual soldier to write home to his family at once and explain what had happened. Our outgoing mail worked fine but the arriving mail did not. It came back with a stamp saying the unit was not in Vietnam.

Uninterrupted mail between a soldier and his loved ones

18

is a matter of the utmost importance to commanders at every level. It goes directly to good morale. Our problem resolved itself quickly once the mail service learned the units in the 3rd Brigade of the 82nd Airborne Division and its subordinate units existed in Vietnam.

I was temporarily assigned to be the brigade's Public Information Officer (PIO). My predecessor had been recently reassigned. I don't know why he was reassigned or where he went. The PIO is a special staff position within the S-1 which is under the supervision of a major. The major was close-lipped about the reassignment, which told me to leave what happened to my predecessor alone. I think my predecessor was fired.

I asked the major why he chose me, who had completed less than sixty college units, to run a small newspaper operation. He told me not to worry; I'd serve for only two weeks while they chose a replacement. I think my performance turned out better than expected because the two weeks stretched into five months.

My duties included supervising a staff sergeant and three Army photographers/reporters, the deployment of the photographers/reporters to cover stories of substantial or potential interest, publishing a monthly newsletter, and later working on putting together a professional quality magazine to be published in Japan.

Fortunately, the staff sergeant was well versed in running a PIO operation. He ran the office while I got a quick but functional education in running a small news operation. I learned a great deal from him. Toward the end of four months, the sergeant and I started the planning for the magazine.

Our primary mission was to report the activities within the brigade's units. We assigned reporters to the battalions engaged in combat operations and actual combat. Although not every mission involved combat with the enemy, we tried to anticipate missions likely to include combat. Combat was always a possibility but not always with a high probability.

Some assignments lacked the luster of combat but played an important role in the plan to win the war. Some were actions to help the Vietnamese people within our area. Others highlighted stories with a human-interest aspect. Ultimately, anything newsworthy got our attention.

The nature of war makes combat stories unpredictable. We sent out reporters to the rifle battalions (Infantry) with missions that offered a chance of combat. Battles became scarcer as the NVA pulled back after its horrendous losses in the Tet Offensive. Years later, the Communist leaders in Hanoi said they lost fifty thousand men and women killed in action during the Tet Offensive. The Viet Cong were virtually wiped out.

A Surprise Reunion

March–April 1968

Being the PIO gave me a great deal of freedom to travel in the Gia Le Combat Base. One day, another classmate and I encountered someone we never expected to see in Vietnam. I knew him as a recent graduate of Infantry Officer Candidate School who'd been assigned as the tactical officer for us in the 2nd Platoon of Officer Candidates in the 97th Student Company, 9th Student Battalion at Fort Benning, Georgia. He'd been a good guy, sort of like a fraternity brother and not too strict with us.

All of us who'd graduated were commissioned as Infantry second lieutenants in a ceremony on November 19, 1967. When we returned to our barracks after the ceremony, he found his orders to Vietnam on his desk. He took it in stride but we who had worked closest with him saw a sort of shock in his face. He wouldn't go immediately though. The Army gives you a thirty day leave before you depart. Plus, his departure date was not for a couple of months. We shook hands and went our separate ways; he stayed with the 97th Company. My comrades and I who had been assigned to the 82nd Airborne Division had orders to report to the Basic Parachute School, then take Christmas leave, and report to the 82nd Airborne Division on Ft. Bragg, North Carolina.

We crossed paths with him somewhere in Gia Le Combat Base. He'd been assigned to the 1st Cavalry Division (Airmobile). Despite the hundreds of helicopters the division had to transport its infantrymen, they did a lot of walking once they exited the helicopters. Walking in the heat, humidity, burdened by the weight of the equipment and weapons he carried during the brief time he'd been in Vietnam had thinned him a great deal.

I was surprised to learn we'd beat him to Vietnam. We weren't supposed to arrive first. We got caught up a little and went our separate ways again. I haven't seen him or heard from him since.

The Brigade's Medical Civic Action Program

My duties weren't always about combat. We reported on planned activities because they had an independent importance. The brigade's MEDCAPS, short for Medical Civic Action Programs, stood head and shoulder above the others. The brigade sent well-supplied medical teams of a physician, medics, an interpreter, and a small security force to the villages in the brigade's Area of Operations (AO). Essentially, the MEDCAP was a huge moving house call.

Each MEDCAP had a simple mission, to provide quality medical diagnoses and treatment to every person in the village. Many of these villagers had never seen a medical doctor, let alone received healthcare from one. We charged them nothing for the visits, the diagnoses, the treatments, the medicines, and the medical supplies we left behind for the treatment regimens the doctor prescribed.

The local Vietnamese genuinely appreciated these "house calls." Subsequent MEDCAPS provided follow-up treatments as the war situation allowed. The Republic of Vietnam awarded the 3rd Brigade a Civil Actions Medal First Class Unit Citation with Palm, in part for these MEDCAPS.

When I was assigned to lead an Infantry platoon, I remembered the MEDCAPS that I accompanied in those early days. I tried to emulate them when the opportunity presented itself, which wasn't often. (See Chapter 8.) My medics stood in for the doctor. In my opinion, the actions we took with the MEDCAPS told the Vietnamese people in the best way possible that we were there to help them and not hurt them.

An NVA Unit Attacks Gia Le Combat Base

May 22, 1968

On the night of May 22, 1968, a unit of the NVA attacked the military unit directly to our left. Both of us were a part of the base's perimeter defenses. The NVA attacked under cover of its own 82mm mortar fire. The NVA soldiers who penetrated the perimeter defenses came armed with AK-47 assault rifles, Rocket Propelled Grenades (RPGs) and demolition charges. They penetrated our neighbor's defenses and reached deep into the area behind its defenses. The NVA killed or wounded a number of the men there. I never learned how many. The NVA also caused considerable damage before being killed or forced out, mostly killed.

During the fight, some of the second lieutenants, including me, lacking assignments for this sort of situation, stood outside our sleeping tent's bunker and looked toward the low ridge that separated us from the automatic weapons firing and the explosions which lay beyond the ridge. Occasional tracers lit up the night sky. At one point, a few RPGs passed over the ridge and headed our way.

RPGs do not come equipped with a tracer element. The red light on the back of one is the flame from a rocket motor. The flame from the RPG coming at me looked softball sized and grew larger as it flew closer. It passed overhead and detonated somewhere behind us, probably on an antenna or guy wire. The brigade headquarters had a number of radio antennae, each with three or four guy wires, in addition to telephone lines running in all directions.

The detonation of an RPG sends a spear of molten metal in the direction the RPG flew and shrapnel in all directions. This got us scrambling to get into the four-man bunker next to our tent.

Complacency in a combat zone will get you killed. I'd left my M-16 in the S-1 tent rather than lug it around. The rockets fired over the ridge at us plus the sounds of AK-47 fire persuaded me to make the risky trip to retrieve my rifle. Guy wires, tent tie down ropes, and tent stakes lay between my rifle and our bunker. On balance, the trip in the dark put me in more danger than staying at the bunker. At the time it seemed the wiser course of action. I didn't repeat this mistake.

I made it safely. I felt a lot better with my rifle in my hands. Fortunately, I didn't have to use it. The enemy attack died within the hour, crushed by the penetrated unit.

The response to the attack included an AH-1 Cobra helicopter gunship newly added to the Army's arsenal and the attack helicopter squadrons in Vietnam. I didn't know one was available. This is the first time I saw one in action.

I saw a stream of tracers pouring from the Cobra like water from a hose. The Cobra gunner fired bursts of varying durations from the Cobra's two six-barreled mini-guns. Each gun fired at a rate of about four thousand rounds a minute at the withdrawing NVA soldiers on the ground. That's a combined rate of fire of eight thousand rounds a minute. It did not consist solely of tracer rounds.

A belt of 7.62 mm machine gun ammunition contains one tracer for every four rounds of ball ammunition. Twenty-six tracer rounds fired every second creates the stream of fire. One hundred thirty-two rounds of ball ammunition and tracers fired every second creates a muzzle flash I estimated as three feet long by one and a half foot high.

The mini-guns emitted a distinct sound when they fired. It reminded me of a large frog's croak but loud enough to hear over the noise of a busy commercial street.

New Orders from the Department of the Army

We received word a few days later from the Department of the Army that it intended to change the brigade's status from Temporary Duty (TDY) to a Permanent Change of Station (PCS). The orders gave individual paratroopers two options; complete six months of TDY and go home to Ft. Bragg or agree to the PCS and stay in Vietnam to complete a regular one-year tour of duty with a one-week Rest and Recuperation (R&R) in a number of locations away from the war.

Those who took option two received a round trip flight to Pope AFB and a thirty-days leave (vacation) followed by returning to complete a one-year tour of duty. The second option had a cutoff date for making a choice. Some of us opted for the six-month tour and return to Ft. Bragg. I expected to hone my skills as the leader of a rifle platoon while waiting for my original projected November departure for a one-year tour.

The cutoff date passed. Subsequently we learned that the Army planned to order us back for a full year tour of duty immediately upon our return from leave. That meant serving a total of eighteen months in Vietnam without the benefits of the first option. Our assignments to S-1 did come with benefits. My friends and I retroactively changed to the second option of staying a complete year in Vietnam.

The reason was simple math. The military used a program of benefits to encourage combat experienced troops to extend a one-year tour by six months. Those who extended became eligible for the program incentives, a "special" off the books thirty-day leave to nearly any place in the world, round trip. It included another one-week out of R&R leave, and a voluntary transfer to the unit of your choice for those six months.

The immediate turnaround under the first option changed our minds. We took the second option. Working in S-1 helped. If any one of us wanted to stay the additional six months, he need only submit the paperwork to garner the special benefits.

I returned to California for my thirty days leave. My family and friends made a little more of it than I did. I assured everyone that I had no intention of getting hurt or doing anything crazy. I didn't know it, but fate had determined something else for me.

I got my personal affairs in order. My uncle had my power of attorney so he could use my checking account to pay my bills. I found out later that my mother had failed to get any of my bills to him. Apparently not having my power of attorney became a sore point with her. My credit rating was more a casualty of the war than I ever was.

I was involved in more activities beyond those of a PIO in the four months after I returned from my leave. Some of my other activities deserve to be called adventures.

Another of my OCS classmates and I took advantage of a lull in our duties to go see his brother, an enlisted soldier with a rank equivalent to corporal. He was assigned to a U.S. Army Radio Research Unit (RRU). This was an electronic eavesdropping operation a few miles outside Gia Le Combat Base. We hitched a ride to get down there.

The brothers tried to have a beer together while they caught up with the personal and family events since they last met face-to-face. The Officer's Club turned us away because the brother was enlisted. The Enlisted Men's Club turned us away because my friend and I were commissioned officers. The Non-Commissioned Officer's (Sergeant's) Club turned all of us away because not one of us was an NCO.

This made no sense. We went to the RRU's headquarters for assistance. The major to whom we related the tale sympathized with the situation but gave us the typical bureaucrat's response: rules are rules or words to that effect. An unwise move as it turned out.

The brother possessed an almanac containing the names and addresses of their U.S. senators and congressmen. Each brother wrote to each asking that this question be investigated, i.e., why can't two brothers in a war zone sit down and have a beer together in at least one of the clubs. The senators and the congressmen sent their own inquiries to the Pentagon. That triggered a formal inquiry through the chain of command to the commander of the RRU.

Each of the Pentagon's communications bore a suspense date, which is the date by which the sender demands to receive a response. Because it came from a much higher-level command it amounted to a direct order, which one disobeys or neglects at one's peril.

In the military, suspense dates are not common and are taken very seriously as I learned a few years later. No, I did nothing wrong. The RRU missed a suspense date or two, which triggered a teletype from the Pentagon demanding a further explanation with a suspense HOUR. Like I said, the military takes suspense dates extremely seriously, particularly when it involves a morale issue like this one.

A few weeks later, we went to visit my friend's brother again. This time the guard at the gate told us to report to the RRU's headquarters. Our escorts quickly ushered us in to see the major we'd met earlier. He apologized for the mix-up about getting into a club. He asked why we had not come to the RRU's headquarters for assistance. We told him we did. He could have said, "I am very sorry for not helping." Instead, he said nothing.

The major personally escorted the three of us to the Officer's Club and presented the brothers with a book of chits covering the cost of their drinks. I bought a beer. We enjoyed talking for a couple of hours. Paratroopers are a tenacious lot. Brash is another way to describe it.

This same classmate had learned of a bar set up by the U.S. Navy Construction Battalion, aka Seabees, in their area of the base. We made a few trips there in the coming months. The main supply route (MSR) made it an easy walk. The hard part came after we left the MSR.

The area contained many short U-channel notched steel posts driven into the ground. They made superb anchors for the closely packed tents and the radio antennas. The force to drive them into the ground left many of them with sharp edges. Unfortunately, the ropes and cables crossed each other creating a maze. The notched steel posts with the sharp edges were angled in different directions. At one point, there was a drainage ditch with a board over it for crossing. The walk was treacherous at night.

My classmate must have made the trip more than once because he knew the safe route to the bar. All I had to do was follow him and try not to trip. The bar was modest, well lighted with simple furnishings. But it was well stocked. We were greeted as comrades. We left after an hour and a couple of drinks. We retraced our steps to the MSR. We made one other trip before my classmate was transferred to an Infantry battalion.

U.S. Air Force Support and Forward Air Controllers

The 3rd Brigade received fighter bomber and Forward Air Controller (FAC) air support from the Air Force's 366th Tactical Fighter Wing, nicknamed "Gunfighters." The Wing was located on Da Nang Air Force Base, during the period I served as the Public Information Officer.

The FACs are brave pilots who fly small fixed-wing aircraft low and slow over enemy territory. They used rockets with white phosphorus warheads to identify enemy targets for ground attack aircraft to attack with guns, rockets or bombs. Indispensable is a good description of their value to us. They saved many an infantryman's life.

One of these pilots spotted an NVA soldier in an open area within our AO. He fired one of his rockets at the NVA soldier, to emphasize a FAC can also kill. He succeeded in freezing the NVA in place. The pilot contacted the 3rd Brigade for assistance. We sent out a small force to take custody of the soldier he had "captured." We made sure that he got the credit for the capture. Not many Air Force pilots are able to claim credit for capturing an enemy soldier.

That pilot was a hero when he returned to Da Nang. We ran a feature article about his actions in the next issue of the brigade's newsletter. We got a copy to him.

One FAC pilot took me along as an observer so I could see what the flight was like. We began with the pilot inspecting the aircraft. Then we took off and headed north.

Somewhere near the halfway point, we came in sight of the FAC who, having finished his morning duty over the 3rd Brigade's AO, headed to Da Nang to rest for a few hours. The two FACs began a mock dogfight. They used rapid clicking of their microphones as a substitute for machine gun fire. This lasted only a couple of minutes before we continued north. I enjoyed this mock dogfight but the word "crazy" did come to mind.

We flew around the brigade's AO for a couple of hours. The first bit was interesting. I was able to see the terrain and mentally compare it with the topographical maps in the brigade's Tactical Operations Center (TOC). It got interesting when the pilot explained that he needed to practice for his periodic flight qualification exam coming in a few weeks.

I remember him stalling the aircraft and recovering a few times. A stall is an aircraft climbing too steeply; it slows and loses its lift, i.e., ceases to fly, and begins to slide backwards towards the ground. Flying in an aircraft falling backwards over terrain in which a concealed enemy lay, is insane. I did not worry much; the pilot had a lot of experience in a variety of aircraft. I found the first one interesting although a little disconcerting despite his expertise.

The pilot finished practicing and flew west to the A Shau Valley. We flew over two or more kilometers of deep stretch of jungle or forest along the base of the eastern side of the high hills on the side of the valley. I say jungle or forest because every bit of plant life was dead and brown. The dead tree trunks stuck straight up like the spikes on the top of wrought iron fences. The Air Force's Operation Ranch Hand had sprayed it with Agent Orange, a powerful defoliant. The devastation ran north and south for kilometers.

It was possible to see the ground between trees, which meant we could also see enemy troop movements. I saw none. Seeing one's enemy makes it easier to capture or kill him. That is the *raison d'être* behind the spraying.

Later the government found out that Agent Orange is a carcinogen. It caused the development of cancers in some United States veterans who marched through or fought in the area. Decades later, a friend of mine from Vietnam died from esophageal cancer caused by Agent Orange.

Flying slowly over the A Shau Valley is more than disconcerting. The area it occupied on our maps should have been annotated with "HERE BE DRAGONS." The NVA owned that bit of land and the hills around it. The valley was the terminus of a branch of the Ho Che Minh Trail, major enemy supply route. It supplied the enemy forces based in and around the valley and north to Khe Sanh south of the Demilitarized Zone (DMZ). The NVA fought fiercely to maintain control of the route and the valley.

The ten-day battle for one hill at the northern end of the valley in May 1969, earned it the name Hamburger Hill. We should have held onto that hill because it blocked supplies and enemy soldiers from entering into A Shau Valley, going east to Hué, and north to Khe Sanh and the Demilitarized Zone (DMZ).

I expected us to come under ground fire any minute but nothing happened. The floor of the valley is flat and wide. It looked like a bomb-cratered packed dirt airstrip or road running down it lengthwise. I saw no signs of the enemy on the heavily forested hills around the valley.

A Major from the 101st Airborne Division Insults My Brigade Commander

One incident deserves mention in any discussion of my time as Public Information Officer. The 3rd Brigade worked under the OPCON of the 101st Airborne Division. Consequently, I had to clear, in advance, the contents of every issue of the 3rd Brigade's monthly newsletter with the 101st's Public Information Officer, a major. At one of those meetings, he informed me that my brigade commander's column was beneath the writing level of a full colonel.

My brigade commander was Colonel Alexander R. Bolling, a soldier with a distinguished combat record dating back to World War II. He led a rifle platoon in one of the waves landing on Omaha Beach. The Germans later captured him. He escaped but was captured again.

He was a damned fine combat leader. The respect of the men of the 3rd Brigade for him, including mine, has not been dimmed by the passage of more than half a century. I served under or with a number of other officers I considered to be good commanders. However, virtually everyone failed to be as proficient. He retired with the rank of major general, a two-star general, a sign of the Army's confidence in his abilities. He passed away many years ago.

This major had just insulted my brigade commander. Military protocol did not permit me, a mere second lieutenant, to voice my opinion of the Major's comment to him. It also did not allow me to inform my brigade commander of his insult unless asked by him or a direct question by an officer superior to me.

Luckily, I swear it was just luck, I crossed paths with Col. Bolling later that day. He asked me how things were going. I figured that was close enough to a direct question to warrant an answer. I explained the situation with that major to him.

Col. Bolling told me to tell that major that he had a master's degree in English, and wrote his column in that manner for the benefit of his soldiers. He wanted his men to understand his message to them since not all of them had received good educations. My colonel told me that if the major had any further questions to come see him personally. His tone of voice, and facial expression, left me with no doubt the major's comment angered him.

I delivered my colonel's message to the major at our meeting the following month. I delivered it pretty much *verbatim*. It's possible that some of my brigade commander's tone came through. Like I said, I respected my boss. As for that major, I had no respect. Call it insubordination if you wish. I prefer contemptuous.

The 3rd Brigade Decimates an NVA Regiment

A part of my job as the brigade's Public Information Office involved attending the evening briefings for Colonel Bolling in the TOC. It was the brigade's war room. Physically, it was a large, fortified, and heavily guarded bunker. The briefings informed him, our subordinate units and the rest of his staff, of our various unit's activities in the field and what the staff sections had been doing. This was where my sergeant and I began our planning for assignment for our reporters/photographers.

The intelligence on enemy actions and movements was always critical information. Tomorrow's planned activities were often a response to what the enemy did. The Colonel gave his guidance to his Operations staff on what he wanted to do about the enemy's movements. By this, I mean his battle plans.

The intelligence part of the briefings began to show steady signs of a substantial enemy presence in the hills some kilometers southwest of the Combat Base's perimeter. Airborne electronic and infrared sensors daily detected signs of a large human presence in multiple locations in the same localized area every day.

Colonel Bolling gave clear orders not to change the aircraft activities over the area and not change the pattern of random artillery firing into it. He told us he did not want to alert the enemy to the fact that we had located them.

This continued for about two or three weeks. Then he sent the Angels of Death, in the form of a reinforced airborne rifle battalion, to destroy them.

The brigade first hit the enemy with coordinated artillery, air, and helicopter gunship attacks. A helicopter air assault by four rifle companies followed. Those four overran the NVA Infantry regiment's positions, captured their regimental communications center including radios and codebooks, and captured the regimental hospital.

These regiments nominally have approximately twenty-five hundred men, including support units, but attrition due to combat losses, non-combat related injuries, and sickness probably had this one down to around thirteen hundred men.

The reinforced battalion captured hundreds of AK-47 assault rifles, SKS rifles, SKS carbines, and dozens of RPD light machine guns, dozens of launchers for rocket-propelled grenades, thousands of rounds of ammunition and hundreds of rocket-propelled grenades.

The last intelligence we had on that regiment said it crossed the DMZ back into North Vietnam with less than two hundred men. The 3rd Brigade's attack destroyed it as a viable combat organization. Curiously, one of the enemy's goals for its Tet Offensive was to destroy one of our brigades. There is a certain irony in the 3rd Brigade turning the tables on them, at least in our small piece of the war. The Army awarded the 3rd Brigade a Valorous Unit Award. The Republic of Vietnam awarded the 3rd Brigade a Gallantry Cross Unit Citation with Palm.

I received an extremely valuable short course of instruction in brigade level combat operations and operational planning. Most second lieutenants do not have that opportunity. It proved useful in the coming months and years.

The work of a Public Information Office requires a certain amount of driving. Unfortunately, the organizational structure of an airborne Infantry brigade did not provide a vehicle for the Public Information Office. Fortunately, I was surrounded with veterans who knew the ropes. On one of my trips to Da Nang we "found" an Army jeep that someone had "lost" or "abandoned."

The brigade's motor pool was kind enough to re-number and re-paint the "found" jeep with a different serial number and the alphanumeric designation for the unit to which it now belonged. They did a great job, which led me to think they did it more often than I ever knew or wanted to know, then or now.

The last time I saw the brigade's motor sergeant, he led some military policemen (MPs) on a merry chase on the packed dirt roads that wound through the brigade area. The MPs drove a stock military jeep with a siren and a blue rotating emergency light. The brigade motor sergeant was in a jeep that had been cut down to a dune buggy. The MPs never caught him. No way could the MPs' stock military jeep catch a jeep dune buggy with a well-tuned and properly adjusted engine.

The monsoon season was ending at the same time we arrived in Vietnam. As summer approached, the day and night temperatures and the humidity rose. While unpleasant at the best of times, the weather turned particularly unpleasant at night. The tent walls and the mosquito nettings for our cots stopped most of the weak breezes from reaching us. I spent many nights sweating while waiting for those occasional breezes that brought the possibility of sleep with them, and it seemed I slept only during the all too infrequent ones.

Roughly once a week the weather gave us a break from the night's heat. Between four and five in the afternoon, the dark clouds of a strong rainstorm front appeared over the eastern hills of the A Shau Valley roughly 64 kilometers (40 miles) to the west. They sped toward us under the pressure of a strong wind. This wind signaled us to drop the sidewalls and end flaps of the Public Information tent to keep out the heavy wind-driven rain.

This anecdote will help to give you some idea of what I mean by heavy wind driven rain. I was busy and failed to notice the signs of the approaching storm. I realized the situation only when I heard the loud and rapid drumming sound the large rain drops made on the tent. I stepped backwards through the tent's doorway to drop the entrance flaps. Without turning, I sidestepped twice to my left to drop the left flap. I then sidestepped four times to my right to drop the right flap. Still not turning, I sidestepped twice to the tent's door and reentered the tent.

I was exposed to the rain for no more than the five to six seconds it took me to drop the tent flaps and step back inside. Only my right side of my uniform had faced the storm and for less than the time it takes to read the first two sentences of this paragraph. On my right side my jungle fatigues were soaking wet with water running from them. The left side was dry except for where the wind blew perhaps a dozen drops of rain.

Thirty minutes later, the storm had passed. The rain beat down the ever-present dust from the combat base's dirt roads. It also cooled the temperature for the remainder of the day and into the night. It left stronger cooler breezes in its wake. That made for good sleeping weather on those nights. The temperature became less of a problem after I became acclimated.

Dust was ever-present during the hot and humid dry season. Early in the dry season, I noticed, within a few hours of taking a shower, I could run my thumb down the inside of my forearm and roll up a tiny ball of mud in the sweat there.

I knew we didn't live the cleanest of lives when I was on staff. It took commanding a rifle platoon in the field for me to see what dirty really meant. We had no clean uniforms for days and no showers for weeks. The best we could do was brush our teeth each day and shave every few days.

I say every few days because the scent from the shaving cream carries some distance with the wind. It was a sure sign of our presence in the area plus our heavy perspiration and the alcohol in the mosquito repellent made any shaving nicks burn. A greater concern was the lack of clean water where we patrolled for the enemy. We could not waste the water we carried with unnecessary shaving.

About four months after I became the PIO, the staff sergeant and I were completing a plan to have a 3rd Brigade magazine printed in Japan. We had reached the point of requiring a trip to Japan to make the necessary arrangements for the printing and shipping of a finished magazine. I planned to get in some shopping for a stereo, to be sent to my home, and a camera or maybe some sightseeing.

About the same time, the major in charge of S-1 informed me my time to lead a rifle platoon had arrived. I was being replaced by a first lieutenant with a college degree. My replacement and the staff sergeant finished the magazine project. The first issue came out not long after I left. Months later I chanced upon an old copy of it. It looked very professional. I didn't get a chance to read it. Still, I heard that it was a great success among the troops.

3

The Brigade's Post Exchange Officer

April 1968 to 26 August 1968

Shortly after my assignment to the brigade's Public Information Office, the S-1's major handed me the additional assignment of Brigade Post Exchange (PX) officer. It was a made-up position and title. A PX is a combination of a department store and a supermarket. It sells food, beverages, clothing, cameras, jewelry and the like to service members and their families.

As PX officer, I possessed a $3,000.00 revolving account to use to purchase beer, soda and canned shoestring potatoes at the PX Depot in Da Nang. I brought the items I purchased to brigade headquarters for later sale to the units assigned to the brigade which replenished the funds for future purchases.

I had to figure out how to accomplish this assignment, starting with obtaining the trucks to transport the goods from Da Nang. I practically begged to borrow the trucks I needed. Since favors are rarely given, I needed to perform an errand for whoever loaned me the trucks or take his people with me, or both. I am not complaining just another challenge to overcome.

Convoys travelling between Phu Bai and Da Nang use Vietnam's National Route 1A. It's a wide two-lane packed red clay road for most of the way. The restrictions on its use presented me with another challenge in fulfilling my role as the brigade's PX officer.

The Marines permitted only northbound convoys on even numbered days. Southbound convoys traveled on odd numbered days.

It could have been the other way around; I never paid much attention to their schedule. These large convoys typically contained a hundred or more vehicles, radio communications from front to rear, and helicopter gunship air cover. Despite these precautions, convoys had been ambushed. The Hai Van Pass was notorious for Viet Cong ambushes.

When I got the trucks I needed, I started south on Route 1A, paying no attention to the odd–even routine. They had their schedule; I had mine. I usually made the round trip once a month or month and a half. If a convoy was headed in the right direction, I followed close behind it. If one approached us head on, or caught up to us (never happened), we pulled to the side and let it pass.

The only real problem was the U.S. Marines guarding the north gate into and out of Da Nang. They enforced the odd–even rule. They did not turn us away if we arrived on the wrong day but they did stop anyone from leaving on the wrong day. I found a way around this challenge.

Once in Da Nang, we went to the Marines' transient quarters. Calling it quarters implies housing, which is too generous a title for a medium size general-purpose tent with two-dozen cots lined up on a sand floor. We only stayed overnight in Da Nang when the time to drive down, buy the tons of beer and soda, and then load it on the trucks created an afternoon start time for the drive back. Starting later risked driving north with little chance of reaching the brigade before nightfall. Worse, it risked our falling victim to an ambush.

Perhaps I was a little crazy, but I was not insane. Things do go bump in the night. You can find them in the Hai Van Pass.

The next day we ate breakfast before going to the depot, an extraordinary place because of its size and contents. I believe it covered four to six acres in size. More to the point, I saw dozens of double-stacked pallets of the various beers, sodas and canned shoestring potatoes sitting within it.

I didn't make ordinary beer runs. Each pallet of beer or soda contained eighty cases of the beverage. Each pallet weighed approximately twenty pounds less than a ton. The shoestring potatoes pallets weighed a lot less. But I was buying beer by the ton!

The weight of the merchandise required using a forklift to lift the one-ton pallets onto the bed of the two-and-a-half-ton truck. Subsequent pallets push previously loaded pallets farther back in the truck bed. Only four pallets fit into the bed of a truck rated to hold two-and-one-half tons. I loaded a single pallet of shoestring potatoes onto a three-quarter ton rated truck which came with the larger truck.

April 16, 1968, the Day the Depot's Forklift Broke Down

Each trip followed this procedure, until the forklift broke down on the trip of April 16, 1968. No viable option existed except to break the steel bands around the pallets I purchased. I formed most of my men into a "human conveyor belt." We hand loaded the cases of beer, soda and snacks onto the trucks case-by-case. I was not happy about making the men work so hard but the cases would not place themselves on the truck. I took a place in the "conveyor belt."

Please take note: no military rule or tradition exists that says a commissioned officer can't get his hands dirty by performing manual labor when necessary!

We'd loaded nearly a half-ton of beer when the depot's yardman got my attention. He'd lost count of how many cases we'd loaded and asked me for the count. Counting pallets is far simpler than counting the individual cases moving quickly along our human conveyor belt. I understood his dilemma.

I had been a science major in college, which required a lot of mathematics. Working with higher-level computations gave me a certain affinity for numbers. I kept a close running count. I told him the count, but almost instinctively dropped twenty cases from the total. He approached me again with the same problem about fifteen minutes later. I dropped twenty more cases from the count.

Meanwhile, I had two of my men, staying out of sight of the yardman, loading the truck cabs with more cases of beer and soda placed under the seats, behind the seats or other spaces big enough to hold a case.

I never had an exact count but I believe that we "liberated" the equivalent of one mixed ton of beer and soda. When we left, we had loaded nearly five tons of the liquids onto the two-and-a-half-ton rated truck and nearly a ton of liquids and snacks onto the three-quarter-ton rated truck. The two-and-a half-ton truck's springs were flat. I had no choice but to overload the trucks. I didn't have enough of them.

We did not "liberate" beer or soda on any other trip. Opportunity rarely knocks twice. Whatever we "liberated" went to the troops. Not a penny went into my pocket or my men's pockets. I suppose I should be ashamed but I'm not; I had a job to do for thousands of paratroopers.

On my first trip to the depot, I heard about an Officer's Club in Da Nang that did not require ration cards to purchase bottles of hard liquor; everywhere else did. I found it. I started buying a mixed dozen of the top brands of scotch, gin, bourbon and rum in quarts each trip. The Club did not carry the smaller fifths.

The prices were low. A quart bottle of twelve-year-old Chivas Regal Scotch sold for $4.25. I traded a bottle of their desired brand to each of the two Marine guards at the gate for passage north on Highway 1A despite the official schedule for convoys. I distributed the remainder around the brigade headquarters to those I thought knew how to put them to good use in trading for things their jobs needed but were difficult to get. Sometimes, I kept one or two for friends or myself. I paid for all of these out of my own pocket, never from taxpayer's monies.

The return trips went along uneventfully with a few exceptions. The April 16 trip was becoming particularly memorable. We fell in behind a convoy headed north to the Hué/Phu Bai area. I appreciated the protection of a real convoy's air cover and communications but I didn't always need it.

A truck tractor hauling a flatbed trailer combination had jack-knifed and overturned where the road ran through the Hai Van Pass. The accident completely blocked the road which was cut into the side of a rather steep hillside. There was no way around it. The convoy halted for a few hours until a truck retriever vehicle arrived to right it. Calling us sitting ducks is an understatement. Happily, nothing happened.

This was a matter of no small concern. The Hai Van Pass was not known as a dangerous place for convoys during the day for nothing. A number had been ambushed in the pass. I'm speaking of convoys with fifty to more than a hundred vehicles. Many men were killed and wounded; many trucks and their cargos were destroyed. To make this a truly perfect day, the passing of the cool, cloudy days of the monsoon had left us sitting on a hot dusty road on a sweltering, humid, and windless afternoon.

Luckily, the truck ahead of us had a refrigerated cargo area. I walked up to it to see if it was carrying something to cool us off a little. I spoke with the senior enlisted man in it. It turned out they were hauling ice cream. None of my men had seen ice cream for months. We quickly came to an arrangement, two cases of beer for a five-gallon container of ice-cold vanilla ice cream. Believe it or not, ice cream was harder to get than the beer.

My men and I only numbered seven soldiers. The chances of us eating five gallons of ice cream ourselves were little to none. In any event, the ice cream melted too fast in the heat. I noticed a couple of small Vietnamese Army trucks behind us. A Vietnamese Army first lieutenant, his wife, their twin daughters, and a driver occupied the lead truck. The second truck was filled with Vietnamese soldiers; their duty was to protect the entire party. The two girls were identical twins. I estimated their age as three years old. I still remember their names, Tau and Thuy pronounced tow, as in how, and twee, if I remember the pronunciation correctly.

All of them suffered from the heat just as we did. I offered some of the ice cream to the Vietnamese lieutenant for his party. Luckily, he spoke some English since I spoke no Vietnamese. We introduced ourselves. His name was Vinh, Chau. Vinh was the family name. He accepted my offer. Both parties lacked the appropriate containers in which to serve the ice cream and utensils with which to eat it. Where there is a will, a way will be found.

Everyone got the equivalent of a large bowl full of ice cream at least, which, in some cases, made for sticky steel helmets. The twins really enjoyed the cold ice cream once they saw it tasted good. I guess ice cream was just as rare in the Vietnamese diet as it was in ours.

I spoke with the lieutenant for a while. He related they were headed to Hué for the funeral of his wife's father, who was killed in the fighting to recapture the city. I also learned the lieutenant commanded a Vietnamese Army Truck Company stationed in Da Nang. He offered me the security of his compound whenever I came to Da Nang, his way of saying thanks for the ice cream.

Before we got under way again, he had our photograph taken. We stood together at the side of the road in the Hai Van Pass. I still have my copy. He looks more professional than me.

The crews finally righted the overturned truck. All of us continued on our individual ways without notable incident. I loved my job.

Accepting Lt. Vinh's Offer and Dinner in a Da Nang Restaurant

I accepted Lt. Vinh's offer the next time I went to Da Nang for beer and soda. His officers took my driver and me to lunch at a fine restaurant at the harbor. It was a pretty nice place. Different from what I was used to, but nice, definitely not a dive.

The food tasted incredibly good. The hors d'oeuvres were crabs cooked in a spiced sauce. They came with thin twelve-inch rounds of rice paper. We used it to wrap the crabmeat and some vegetables into something like small burritos. Two different dipping sauces came with the meal—simply dip and enjoy. The best one was a delicious warm spiced lemon sauce. The other was fermented fish oil. Its taste remains unknown to this day.

The main course was a large sea catfish. The protocol for it was identical to the way to eat the crab hors d'oeuvres and just as tasty. This was a delicious meal. The company was good despite the language barrier. The Vietnamese Tiger Beer was passable.

I often wonder how Lieutenant Vinh and his family fared after the Communist North's victory, especially the fates of the twins. I never saw him, his wife or the twins after the end of my six months on brigade staff. I hope they were spared any retribution or hardship after the North Vietnamese conquered South Vietnam.

My First Near Death Experience

My first close call with death from enemy action happened on one of my other trips to Da Nang. We were staying overnight at the transient tent the Marines provided. My cot sat three feet from the front wall of the tent. The edge of the two-lane roadway, about thirty feet wide, lay a further four feet beyond the tent wall. After dark, a marine parked a five-ton truck at the edge of the road and directly in front of the tent.

The Marines' administrative office, made of plywood, stood on the far side of the road. It was set back about twenty-five feet from the far edge of the road. Our tent sat between two other identical tents all set side by side. A small plywood building sat on the far side of the tent on our right. It faced the road.

The VC or the NVA fired some 122 mm rockets into the Marine base during the night. The ones passing over my head generated a kind of whistle when they passed. The longer the whistle the further away they struck. The shorter the whistle the closer the point of impact. The Marines sporadically returned fire with their artillery for the remainder of the night.

At daybreak, the enemy fired a single 122 mm rocket into the Marine base, I think to say, "You missed me." They probably laughed too. I know in their place I'd have been laughing too.

I was awake, sitting on the street side edge of my cot when I heard the briefest of whistles of a 122 mm rocket passing close overhead, literally a split second in length. I instantly knew what was coming. Just as instantly I acted. It happened too fast to remember the details. I somehow jumped over my cot and away from the tent front. I landed on the sand about six feet further away from the road.

I was trying to put as much distance as possible between what was coming and me.

I was not quick enough. The rocket struck the opposite side of the street, a distance of about forty to forty-five feet from where I lay. When it exploded, it became the loudest explosion I had ever heard. It was even louder than the one in Chu Lai because it was right on top of me versus a mile or more away.

Miraculously, I did not get injured in the blast. I was spared injury from the explosion's concussion wave too. I checked on my men. All but one was okay. He had new skin on his face growing back from a flash fire of loose pieces of mortar propellant. The new skin split a little when his chin hit the sand diving away from the blast. Otherwise, he was fine.

I went outside through the tent entry to survey the situation and render whatever aid was needed. I was met with a scene of destruction. The rocket dug a shallow impact crater a few feet beyond the far edge of the street directly in front of the Marine administrative office building's entrance. The explosion propelled hundreds of pieces of shrapnel and small rocks through the front wall of the building. There were no casualties because the Marines had not yet arrived for work. But this was not the end to the destruction.

The rocket's back blast partially blew down half of the tent to my right beginning with the end fronting on the street. I saw no signs of shrapnel holes but I had no doubt it had many. The back blast also partially blew down the small plywood building on the far side of that tent. The wall facing the blast, while still standing, was shot through with rock and shrapnel holes. The street end of the tent to my left was also partially blown down. Again, I did not see any shrapnel holes but I knew it had more than a few.

My tent was undamaged despite being almost directly across the street from the detonation. More importantly, not one of my men had a scratch from the explosion, regardless of what surrounded us. How was that possible? The five-ton truck parked right in front of our tent is how.

No vehicle had ever been parked there on any other night that I spent in that tent. Shrapnel from the backblast had heavily damaged the truck on the driver's side. It had shredded half of the four pairs of dual rear tires under the bed of the truck. A couple on my side survived. The truck sagged in the rear.

The truck had absorbed all of the rocket's back blast and shrapnel that was headed in the direction of my men and me. The distance from where I sat on my cot to the far side of the truck was a mere fifteen or sixteen feet. I am sure my men would have been grievously wounded if someone had not parked the truck in that precise spot. Being closest to the explosion, I would have been shredded like the truck's tires. This may be why I have such a strong memory of that morning.

You can call it luck or Divine Intervention or whatever you like, but we escaped unscathed because on that night someone parked a five-ton truck in front of our tent. I still wonder if Someone was watching out for us that morning.

My Second Near Death Experience

In the next convoy to Da Nang I rode in a jeep driven by a Medical Services first lieutenant. I didn't know him well but I had encountered him several times around headquarters. I sat in the right front seat, literally riding shotgun, except I carried a loaded M-16A1. Somewhere about the midpoint of the trip south I began feeling increasingly ill and dizzy. The dizziness came upon me quickly and was a prelude to a loss of consciousness. As I drifted into unconsciousness I started to fall out of the jeep. It is easy enough; they lack doors.

I remember I had involuntarily rotated in my seat until my head and upper back were outside of the jeep and the flat of my back was parallel to the road surface. I looked straight up at the sky without needing to turn my head. I knew I was in trouble but I lacked any ability to help myself. My last conscious thought was marveling at a huge hand reaching out for me and pulling me back into the jeep. I lost consciousness for the rest of the drive. How the Medical Services lieutenant pulled me back and maintained control of a jeep traveling at 25+ miles per hour on a dirt road remains a mystery to me.

I regained consciousness that night. I was in a dark military tent. The American voices and uniforms told me I was in Da Nang. I did not think about the time or remember that I wore a watch. I had no idea how much time had passed.

I did know I lay on a cot in terrible pain, burning up with fever and in my sweat-soaked fatigues. I drifted in and out of consciousness. Everything remained the same from conscious period to conscious period. All I can say is time passed but I don't know how much.

It was still dark when I staggered to a nearby latrine (outhouse) visible because the sidewalls of the tent had been rolled up. The agony of the trip was nearly unbearable. I had second thoughts before each subsequent trip. Strangely, I knew I wasn't in a hospital but didn't worry about this. I felt disconnected from reality in my thoughts during those hours.

I finally woke in the morning. The Medical Services first lieutenant came for me. I was hungry, not starving hungry, just hungry. My fever had broken. I felt like I had been running at full speed for days and had used up every bit of energy in my body. He must have taken me to where I could get something to eat and drink. I do not remember where or what. But I recovered more with the food and drink.

When he finished getting the medical supplies for which he had come, we headed north to Phu Bai. I think I slept on the trip back because I remember nothing about it or arriving in the brigade area. I returned to my normal duties in a few days. I still have no idea what had made me sick. Thankfully, I've had no recurrences. For the record, neither alcohol nor drugs were involved.

More Opportunities in Da Nang

The trips to Da Nang offered many opportunities. I saw that the Marine Corps took very good care of its officers. I walked through the unoccupied dining room of the Officer's Club. I was surprised to see tables covered with white linen tablecloths. Each table had its complement of matching well-upholstered padded armchairs. Being focused on reaching the bar to obtain something to clear the red clay dust from my throat, I gave it no further thought.

Less than half a dozen officers sat in the bar in the early afternoon. Two Marine officers entered not long after I did. They made two facts clear. First, their orders to go home had arrived. Second, they were buying the drinks. That was fine with me, except I was not used to drinking a lot. I remember seeing six untouched drinks sitting on the bar in front of me.

I tried to keep drinking to avoid offending them. But I knew when I reached my limit. I'd probably passed it. I congratulated them, thanked them for the drinks, and bid *adieu* to them and the other bar patrons. I left to retrace my footsteps through the dining room. I left those six or seven untouched drinks on the bar.

Upon seeing those armchairs again, I was suddenly reminded of seeing my brigade commander sitting on an Army issue, visibly uncomfortable, unpadded, folding wooden chair in his tent. Blurry thought instantly followed blurry thought. I thought he deserved a padded and upholstered armchair. The time between thought and action was a microsecond. I hoisted one of those chairs onto my shoulder and walked out with it.

When I returned to Phu Bai, I delivered it to the brigade commander sergeant major to replace the colonel's uncomfortable Army issue chair. The CSM, being a fine soldier and gentleman, did not ask how I came by it. I asked that my name not be mentioned; I sought no favor or special treatment.

My storage unit for the beer and soda was a shipping container, made of heavy gauge steel, half the size of the usual containers one sees on trailers near ports or on highways and securely padlocked. It rested in one of the safest places possible, outside the brigade's TOC, which was guarded at all times. Beer and sodas were hard to come by despite the quantities I bought. No one ever attempted to steal from my inventory.

My assistant and I stood next to the container a couple of weeks before one of the trips to replenish my stocks. Col. Bolling walked up to me. After exchanging salutes and greetings, he told me two of our companies had been engaged in a major firefight outside of Hué.

They won the battle. Now he wanted to send them some beer and soda in a show of his appreciation for their performance and efforts.

I told my assistant to count out ten cases of beer, ten cases of soda and ten cases of canned shoestring potatoes for each company. The Colonel told me the brigade would pay for it. Of course, I thanked him, but I added that was not necessary as the cost was covered. This was after April 16's trip. He simply looked at me for a second or two. I knew he was wondering how I, a green second lieutenant, could give away beer and soda for free. Being a fine soldier and gentleman, he didn't ask the obvious question.

He knew the answer. Of that, I have not the slightest doubt.

He gave me the details for delivery; we exchanged salutes again and he left. Anyone else would have had to pay. He called me Mike. I'd never shared that name with him. Yet he knew I used my middle name. I assume he asked someone. I interpreted that to mean he saw me as more than another bit of cannon fodder. I realized if he saw me that way, he saw every paratrooper in the brigade the same way. Knowing your commander will not throw your life away makes for excellent morale.

But I was bound more by notions of respect than military regulation to refer to him as sir or colonel and later general. I always did. I was proud of him and proud to serve under him! Months later I saw him interact with the men in my rifle platoon. I saw him let his men know that he cared about them and would never let them down.

That may sound like hero worship. Maybe it is. But I knew from watching his command style, he planned his battles to get the job done while losing the fewest men as humanly possible to injury or death. A class in OCS drilled a similar concept into us.

Army doctrine states an officer's first priority is to accomplish his mission. His second is the welfare of his men, which I understood to mean keeping them alive and well. Most of the time a commander can complete the mission and see to the welfare of his men simultaneously. Always keeping in mind, "The best laid schemes o' mice an' men Gang aft a-gley [often go awry]" (from Robert Burns' poem "To a Mouse").

It's not easy to give orders that will almost certainly result in deaths or horrible wounds to men you marched with through swamp and jungle for months and know well. Adhering to these precepts helps to ease the pain, which comes with responsibility, but only a little.

I had tremendous confidence in Col. Bolling and one other officer's ability (discussed in Chapter 17) as a military commander because each led with his mission in mind and the welfare of his men constantly. If you think like this long enough, it becomes second nature. I did my best to emulate both. I learned the price a leader must pay despite making every effort to take care of his men. You never forget the men killed or wounded under your command.

Calling Home on the Military Affiliated Radio Station

The Marine Base at Da Nang had a MARS Station. Its formal title is Military Affiliated Radio Station otherwise known as a ham radio setup. I used it sometimes whenever I stayed overnight in Da Nang. The operator contacted a ham radio operator in the United States to set up a patch for a collect telephone call to whomever you wanted. I signed up early in the evening and waited for it to go on the air at eleven p.m. I let the other men go ahead of me until I knew it was time for my family to be getting ready for school or work.

I wanted to assure them I was still alive. We only had minutes to get caught up with the news from each other before ending the call. I also liked to surprise them, get them excited and off their game plans for the rest of the day. The important point is they heard my voice.

I had no one else to call. I had severed most of my ties when I got my commission. I knew a trip to Vietnam lay in my future. Infantry lieutenants are taught to lead their men into battle. We do not send them into battle. We lead them! Leading is a great place from which to direct the battle but it is not the safest of places to be in a firefight. This explains why there are always vacancies for Infantry lieutenants needing filling.

I had seen firsthand what happens to those we leave behind

when they get that terrible knock on the door. I did not intend for a girlfriend, fiancée or wife to suffer that.

Redeployment to the Capital Military District Around Saigon

26 August to 30 October 1968

The 3rd Brigade had received orders to move to the Capital Military District around Saigon. We would begin the move in three weeks beginning August 26. Getting to lead a rifle platoon had to wait until the actual deployment began. About the same time, an S-1 major informed me my transfer was to the 1st Battalion, 505th PIR. I responded in the only way possible, "Yes Sir." I followed that with, "Col. Bolling told me I could pick my battalion when my time came to go to the field." The tent got quiet. The major was not happy. Finally, he asked for the battalion I wanted. "1st of the 508th Sir."

I got my wish. The Colonel did say that to me some weeks earlier. I did not like using his words but I had a good friend from OCS in the 508th.

Instead of seeking out large NVA units in the rolling hills around Hué, my mission would become searching for small Viet Cong units in the rice paddies west of Saigon.

I received the Army Commendation Medal for my service as the 3rd Brigade's Public Information officer and Post Exchange Officer.

4.

Transferred to the
1st Battalion, 508th PIR

26 August 1968 to 30 October 1968

"Executive Officer" Headquarters, 1st Battalion, 508th PIR

One of my classmates from OCS and the Airborne School was transferred from brigade headquarters to D Company of the 508th months earlier. I had hoped for an assignment to the same rifle company. I was transferred to the 508th because Col. Bolling told me to pick my battalion. That is a one-time privilege.

Never before did I experience the value of knowing people in high places. It was something that made me feel a little uncomfortable. I never used it again although I benefited from it two more times in the coming months, nothing earthshaking though.

Instead of combat with NVA units to engage in the open country and rolling hills around Hué or the A Shau Valley, my mission would become endless searches for the Viet Cong in a postage-stamp sized area of rice paddies west of Saigon.

My luck continued to hold. D Company was returning to the battalion's rear area. It was to participate in a change of command ceremony at the headquarters of the 101st. My transfer to D Company was guaranteed.

Commanding the Battalion's Defense Perimeter at Night for Nine Weeks

I was transferred to Headquarters Company of the 1st Battalion of the 508th nine weeks prior to the redeployment. I moved my gear to Headquarters Company while I awaited the return of D Company to the rear area. The battalion's area happened to be at the base of the ridge about which I spoke earlier. I was made the "executive officer" of Headquarters Company. It was another made-up position. A battalion's headquarters company is not allotted an executive officer.

As my primary function, I commanded the battalion's defense perimeter's defensive bunker line for those nine weeks. It's an all-night job. It lasted until the battalion's rifle companies returned for the transfer to the Saigon area in III Corps. The unit to the left of our bunker line was the one the NVA penetrated on May 22.

The terrain beyond our perimeter defenses consisted of low, virtually bare rolling hills with innumerable creases like gullies and ravines. Great distances separated occasional trees or bushes. A scattering of sparse low vegetation and pebble size rocks covered the hard ground.

The bunker line sat on the downward slope of a small saddle between the end of the ridge on our left and a low hill to our right. Several rows of concertina wire, which is a barbed wire coiled like a spring, stretched laterally in front of the bunkers. Some of the rows were stacked in a pyramid, with one row on top of two.

We festooned each row of concertina wire with empty C-ration cans containing a few pebbles. An enemy crawling through the concertina wire could not avoid shaking the cans and making a loud rattling noise. The idea was to alert us to the enemy's presence no matter how dark or rainy the night.

The slope continued down about fifty feet to a crease in the ground. The far side of the crease rose to become another hill with more hills beyond it for miles. The rows of concertina wire reached about halfway down the slope to the crease.

Our engineers prepared some nasty surprises for uninvited guests. They emplaced some empty 55-gallon steel drums and expended 105 mm artillery casings on the friendly side of the concertina wire. The open ends pointed away from us at an angle of 45 degrees toward the hill across the crease.

The surprise in each of them was jellied gasoline. We called it "Foo Gas." The rest of the world called it napalm. A rose by any other name, etc. The engineers mixed a thickening agent with gasoline to make it. A large explosive charge at the bases of the drums and casings launched the jellied gasoline into the air and spread it out over the concertina and the slope like a heavy mist. A smaller explosive charge, detonated a fraction of a second later, ignited the gasoline. It's a very effective defense.

A dirt road at the right end of the bunker line led through a reinforced barbed wire gate in the concertina wire. The road followed the tiny valley to the right, then disappeared between the low hills and the brigade's other perimeter defenses.

Rifle fire and a 106 mm recoilless rifle covered the gate and the road. A recoilless rifle is a small cannon which uses its back blast to counter the recoil. It fired projectiles filled with hundreds of one inch long, finned steel darts or flechettes. We kept it pointing at the reinforced gate and down the road.

It was loaded with a flechette round. These are dial-a-range rounds. This one was dialed to muzzle action. The hundreds of flechettes would spread as they left the barrel, killing anyone near the gate and on the road. A second round would do the same across the slope and the triple concertina wire.

We had formidable defenses but history is replete with formidable defenses that failed. Well-known examples include the walls of Troy and the Maginot Line but for different reasons.

The dirt road passed a makeshift rifle range about a hundred yards from the gate. Further to the right, it ran parallel with the perimeter, continued a short distance to vanish in the low hills.

Those small valleys, gullies and ravines between the low hills offered excellent, concealed, and protected avenues of approach to our perimeter. Most of the hills had almost nothing in the way of large foliage. Anyone crossing them risked exposure from backlighting upon reaching the crests. Large units could remain out of sight only by staying in the gullies and ravines. This fact became painfully clear to our neighboring unit on our left when the NVA penetrated their perimeter defenses on May 22, 1968.

Nevertheless, the country is beautiful to see in daylight or under a moon in a starlit night sky. I made several forays out there, some in daylight, most at night because I needed to know the dangers the terrain held for me. The night forays involved simple observation or listening posts.

A field telephone served as my primary means of communication at the bunker line. It provided me with contact to Headquarters Company or with the TOC. We received two sets of an experimental compact radio sometime later. Each set consisted of a receiver which clipped onto a steel helmet and a handheld transmitter. It was like those two-piece telephones you see in the black and white movies from the 1920s and '30s, except the telephones worked.

The radio suffered from three problems, only one frequency, short range, and it did not work. Allegedly, the radios could communicate within a range of about a quarter of a mile. I felt thrilled on the rare occasions I contacted the other radio at a hundred yards. I did better by yelling.

I occasionally got my hands on hand-launched parachute flares or a white star cluster. I used them to illuminate the nearby terrain exposing any enemy forces there. If any showed up some distance away, I intended to order the two soldiers with me to go quietly and quickly to our defensive perimeter with orders to put it on a silent full alert and notify the battalion and brigade headquarters of the situation. I would follow them at a distance for their protection.

If the enemy presented an imminent threat to our perimeter, the three of us would engage the enemy with rifle fire and break contact with grenades, then run like hell back to the bunker line to verbally report the enemy's presence and location in case the rifle fire and exploding grenades went unnoticed. I'm sure the noise we made would alert everyone in the area to the danger, but common sense says make sure the message gets through.

I used parachute flares and white star clusters to illuminate an unseen enemy or cause him to withdraw, essentially scare him away after being possibly discovered. I found the star cluster is best for this. Both rockets make a loud noise, a sort of popping sound when it ejects its payload at the peak of its trajectory. The flare does not ignite for a second or two, time enough for a trained soldier to conceal himself before the flare lights up. The star cluster instantly illuminates a large area with the pop.

Those low empty hills separated us from the much higher hills on the eastern edge of the A Shau Valley to the west. The A Shau Valley sat at the terminus of the northernmost branch of the Ho Chi Minh Trail. It fed a constant supply of soldiers, weapons including artillery, ammunition, medical supplies and food into the battles south of the Demilitarized Zone (DMZ) and southward thirty to forty kilometers to the A Shau Valley. From there, they headed our way.

The main branch of the trail continued south along the Vietnam-Laos and Vietnam-Cambodia borders to the mouth of the Mekong River. Small branches split off along the whole trail to bring reinforcement and supplies to the enemy forces eastward across Vietnam to the South China Sea. It always presented a serious threat to us. Especially when we moved to our new AO west of Saigon.

The men assigned to nighttime perimeter duty came from the rear elements of the 508th's rifle companies and from Headquarters Company, mostly clerks, cooks or men coming from or returning to the companies in the field. The make-up changed nearly every night. One semi-regular "volunteer," a specialist 4, essentially a corporal, became my non-commissioned officer in charge, not quite a formal designation. I told the night's crew to obey him if I was not around for some reason. If the bunker line began to receive fire, everyone in the battalion rear area reinforced us.

I did not trust our defenses. They were similar to those of the unit to our left. Also, no defensive measures existed for us to stop an attack by men willing to die so their comrades get through, i.e., a human wave attack.

This is why I undertook small patrols outside the perimeter during the waning minutes of twilight and into the night. It's the one tactic I could use to better our chances and worsen theirs. The three soldiers I took with me would quietly sit listening for the sound of a moving force of enemy soldiers' movements in nearby gullies and ravines or watching the skylines of the hills for backlit NVA soldiers. In the quiet nights, sounds like a shod foot scraping the pebbled hillsides and gullies carried a long way.

I knew those men were concerned about their safety. For this reason, I chose the walled enclosures of the few Vietnamese graves in the hills for our observation posts when possible. I also needed their additional eyes and ears as we roved over the hills or sat watching and listening. Six eyes and ears see and hear more than two.

Each of us provided a small measure of mutual support to the others. I usually stayed out between one to two hours but not every night. Nothing was repetitive. Setting a routine could get my men and myself killed.

On the nights I took the men out, I patrolled anywhere from half a kilometer to a kilometer out and half that laterally. Once, I located the site from which an NVA mortar crew launched about a dozen 82 mm mortar rounds into the base months earlier, probably May 22. They left behind the packaging holding the mortar bombs. I have no idea why someone did not detect them before they launched mortar bombs. Perhaps no one looked.

I never came across anything or anyone else. Lacking reliable communications, I would need to send one or both men back to get word to the bunker line with a warning of an enemy force nearby. I think the reason I never saw any signs of enemy forces headed our way was the horrific losses in their Tet Offensive. They didn't have the manpower.

I thought about the kinds of situations I might encounter. From this, I worked out the appropriate actions to take. I found it better to plan early rather than wait until events overtook me, with no time to plan. I did the same when I commanded my platoons. The Army has a phrase, which beautifully captures the "why" behind planning: "Prior Planning Prevents Piss Poor Performance." The 6 P's are true. My basic plan was simple: send one or both men back to the bunker line to report the situation to headquarters and sound a full alert for our battalion rear.

If we discovered an NVA mortar crew setting up to fire into the Base Camp, I had only one option, send one man back with a warning while the other paratrooper and I opened fire to kill the mortar crew. Mortar fire posed an immediate danger of friendly casualties. He and I would enjoy the element of surprise and perhaps the advantage of higher ground.

One starry well-lit night, as we returned from one of these patrols, we reached the bend where the road turns left toward the gate in the perimeter. I saw the bunker line was in an alert status. Everybody hunched in the communication trenches or bunkers with their weapons pointed at the area to their front. We happened to stand to their front. Lacking radio communications with them, I wanted to try yelling to them, reconsidered the idea and instantly discarded it. Startling them with a loud yell seemed unwise.

I became concerned by the distinct possibility we could be mistaken for the enemy. We moved slowly into the open, with no sudden moves. We made it to the gate without incident. It turned out the paratrooper I'd left in charge ran along the communication trench between the bunkers telling each man we were friendlies and not to fire. I hope he survived to go home and realize his dreams.

I never heard what caused the alert. I know my patrol did not cause it. You hear about those things from higher ranked officers.

A Typhoon and Three Days Soaking Wet and Cold

Only one other problem arose during the time I ran the bunker line. A typhoon (the name for a hurricane in Asia) hit us with extremely heavy rain and winds for three days. It flooded the bunkers and the communication trenches connecting the bunkers.

To give you an idea of what it felt like: I returned to my tent one morning to get some sleep and discovered a stream now ran through the tent and under my cot. While an interesting phenomenon, the stream became part of the reason why the typhoon took all the romance out of standing, sleeping, or walking in the rain. We spent three days soaking wet and cold.

The cooks did praiseworthy work to take care of us during the typhoon. They erected a medium tent not far behind the bunker line and set up a field kitchen in it. They kept fresh sandwiches, hot soup and hot coffee ready for my men throughout the three miserable nights. I rotated the men back to the tent as often as possible while leaving the battalion's perimeter adequately defended.

During those cold and wet nights, I learned a cup of hot soup possesses a truly magical property. It temporarily drives away the worst effects of being out in a miserable cold rainy night. Perhaps this is the reason why to this day I relish a good soup or stew.

The Brigade Is Transferred to the Saigon Capital Military District in III Corps

Life in Phu Bai in the 508th continued in a normal fashion until the brigade received orders to begin transferring to the Capital Military District surrounding Saigon. The benefit for me was to take command of D Company's 1st Platoon. We made the trip by air in Air Force C-130s; they're the workhorses of logistic operations within a theater of war like Vietnam.

The brigade's paratroopers were familiar with them. We made many parachute jumps from these aircraft. My "cherry" jump, the first one after training, was out of a C-130 at Ft. Bragg.

By any measure, the flight to Tan Son Nhut Air Base, near Saigon, was not ordinary. We sat on large square steel pallets about fifteen feet by fifteen feet. The Air Force cargo master packed us tightly to accommodate the largest number of soldiers. Once again, we looked reminiscent of sardines packed tightly together in tins. The tight packing minimized the number of flights necessary to move the entire brigade, reduced the time to accomplish the move, reduced the cost, and maximized our discomfort.

The C-130 possesses neither the comfort nor the panache of the C-47. Don't take me wrong. The C-130 is a great aircraft. I just prefer the much smaller C-47 for its comfort and timeless dignity.

5

1st Platoon, D Company, 1st Battalion, 508th PIR

30 October 1968 to 20 March 1969

Pre-Transfer Briefing on the Enemy Situation in the Battalion's New AO

We were briefed on the battalion's new AO. It contained approximately 250 local force VC. The battalion could easily handle a force of that size. Then the briefer went on to tell us to expect reinforcements of 6,000 VC soldiers within forty-eight hours! Now there's a game changer. The force difference at the Little Big Horn comes to mind. A difference which certainly worked out well for the 7th Cavalry, didn't it? The 6,000 never made their presence known. Years later we learned they'd been nearly wiped out during their part of the Tet Offensive.

D Company Is the Reaction Force to Defend or Retake the United States Embassy

D Company was given the contingent mission to support the 11th Armored Cavalry Regiment (ACR) in the event of another Tet Offensive. We were to enter Saigon to defend the American embassy or the American ambassador's residence. D Company's officers received briefings from the Operations and Intelligence Officers of the 11th ACR once we'd gotten settled near Saigon.

A distant photograph of a possible Saigon rooftop for a helicopter landing site should D Company be deployed to defend the U.S. Embassy or the Ambassador's residence, 1968.

In the event of another Tet-like offensive in Saigon, D Company would be placed under the OPCON of the 11th ACR with the mission to defend the United States embassy or the ambassador's residence. It depended on where the ambassador was physically located. In the worst-case scenario, we would be ordered to retake one or the other of them.

We went on a tour of the area around the embassy and the residence to see the known points and routes the Viet Cong forces employed in Tet '68 to attack the embassy. A key part of the tour involved locating possible helicopter landing sites for us. I used the word sites instead of the more common "zone" because we did not locate a site large enough to accept more than one aircraft at a time. The history of war tells us piecemeal entry into battle risks destruction of each piece as it arrives.

The rooftops of tall buildings served as landing sites because most of them were large enough for one UH-1 helicopter to land at a time. We found a few available parks but using them left us too far

59

from the embassy to be effective. My platoon alone would require six or seven landings. D Company would need between twenty-five and thirty landings for four platoons and the company command element. It would take up to an hour to insert all of us. Less if we used multiple rooftops.

A distinct possibility existed that we could find ourselves fighting in a series of street battles to reach the embassy or the ambassador's residence. This meant fierce battles with the certainty of heavy casualties.

Kit Carson Scout, interpreter and former VC assigned to 1st Platoon, D Company, 1968.

The intricate façade of the building across from the embassy offered the VC dozens of firing positions well protected by the façade. They could bring automatic weapons and RPG fire directly onto the embassy. In that situation, D Company's mission would change to clearing the VC from that building. The briefing about our role in protecting the embassy caused me to make a major change in my armament. The ten magazines in my ammo pouches, a fifth magazine in the cover of each four-magazine pouches, would not last through a prolonged firefight or series of firefights. I anticipated getting resupplied would be difficult if not impossible. From

Abandoned house with scallions near the village of Vinh Binh in the rice paddies west of Saigon, 1968.

an infantryman's perspective, retaking the embassy is one of those "come as you are" events.

Increasing the Amount of Ammunition I Carried

The prospect of street battles in Saigon convinced me to increase the number of loaded magazines I carried. The ammunition for our M-16s came from the factory in ten round clips, two each in the seven pockets in a cloth bandolier. I repurposed two bandoliers. I replaced the twenty rounds of M-16 ammunition in each pocket with a loaded magazine. It worked. I know it seems obvious but the middle of a firefight is not the time to be loading magazines.

I could use the extra magazines myself in a firefight or toss an entire bandolier to those running low on ammunition. I began wearing those two cloth ammunition bandoliers crisscrossed over my chest. This gave me an appearance like one of Pancho Villa's soldiers but lacking the big mustache. I carried four hundred and fifty rounds of M-16 ammunition in twenty-five magazines. I did not fill the magazines completely, in order to prevent the springs in them becoming too weak to push the rounds up.

I also carried two fragmentation grenades, two smoke grenades of different colors for marking our location for helicopters and air support, and a hunting knife I kept sharp enough to shave with taped upside down on the left shoulder strap of my load bearing harness. I wore this harness on my person. I carried additional ammunition and one Claymore directional anti-personnel mine in my rucksack. I am not a "Rambo" but I am a pragmatist.

The Claymore mine is a command-detonated device designed to protect us in our position of the moment. It is about eight inches long, five inches high and an inch and a half thick. Its legs hold it about three inches above the ground. It is slightly curved, making it directional. The curve serves two purposes. First, it spreads the seven hundred and sixty ball bearings widely and evenly. It fires those ball bearings generally in the direction to which the curve points. It is an effective defense weapon and deadly or crippling out to fifty or more feet. Secondly, it can be rigged as a booby trap.

I estimate the total weight of all that plus three days of food and water, my personal gear, my M-16A, one steel helmet, bedding, and poncho, was something like seventy to eighty pounds.

Patrolling the Rice Paddies in Saigon's "Rocket Belt"

Prior to the move to the new AO, we received briefings on the area, its different geography and the different enemy. The area was predominantly flat. A few hills lay many miles to the west. Unlike the uninhabited hills south of Hué, the new area held villages of various sizes surrounded by flat land filled with rice paddies interspersed with the occasional small copse of trees, and an abandoned cement block home of a better off farmer. The main village in our AO ran one kilometer long by a third of a kilometer wide.

I found the enemy situation portion of the intelligence briefing interesting, as in the old misattributed Chinese curse, "May you live in interesting times." It came from an English politician making reference to the stresses of the early 20th century.

Leading D Company's 1st Platoon, my first command of a manned platoon, made me nervous. I imagine I appeared a bit stiff to them. Fortunately, I'm a quick learner. Little by little we became accustomed to working with each other.

Initially, we patrolled Saigon's suburbs. It rained every day, making every day miserable. The suburbs consisted of better built versions of the thatched huts I would see when the 508th entered our primary AO. We patrolled the suburbs for about two weeks to get acclimated, if acclimated means constantly wet.

The 508th's AO, primarily villages surrounded by rice paddies, lay beyond the western edges of Saigon. This area fell within Saigon's "Rocket Belt." The Viet Cong launched 122 mm (4.8 inch) rockets into Saigon from the Rocket Belt. Our mission tasked us to prevent this happening, not an easy task when you think about it.

The VC used an efficient, quick, improvised system to launch a few rockets at a time. Intercepting them occupied much of my time there. They sneaked into a firing position under the cover of darkness. Once there, they propped up the rockets with bamboo poles in an "X" shape and aimed them in the direction of Saigon or Tan Son Nhut Air Base.

They fired the rockets by using a clever field-expedient electric timing mechanism. They'd use a battery with one pole connected to a metal bowl with a little water in it and the other pole connected to a small piece of metal on a thin piece of wood. When the ambient heat caused the evaporation of enough water, the piece of metal on the wood touched the metal bowl, completed the circuit and fired the rocket. I doubt the emplacement of a rocket took longer than three minutes. The key factor for the VC was they didn't need to wait. No rockets were fired from our AO while D Company patrolled it. We never saw, let alone engaged, any enemy forces either.

We each received one-quart bladders to increase the amount of potable water we carried in our canteens. I carried two, which meant the weight of an extra half gallon of water. I included this weight in the eighty pounds. The total may be greater. We never weighed our gear.

Sometimes I found it difficult to rise from a sitting position when wearing my gear. I usually stood up without the rucksack, grabbed one of the shoulder straps and slung the rucksack up and around until the shoulder strap slipped over my shoulder. From that point, it was like putting on a coat, albeit a very heavy coat. When I did not get it right the rucksack swung me around.

Our New Artillery Forward Observer

We received a replacement Forward Observer (FO) from our supporting artillery, Battery C, 2nd Battalion, 321st Field Artillery. Battery C deployed with the 508th. It was equipped with six 105 mm (4.1 inches) Towed Howitzers. Unlike the FO who deployed with the brigade the newly arrived second lieutenant was not airborne qualified. We referred to the not airborne qualified as a "Legs" because they "legged" it into combat while we flew to the battlefield and parachuted down.

The FO flew with D Company's Officers on an aerial reconnaissance of our new AO. I saw my company commander slip the helicopter pilot a note. Soon, it became obvious he asked the pilot to give the new guy a "good" flight. Our sense of humor was a typical guy thing, hard on each other but with no malice. We flew about a thousand feet above the ground but sometimes the pilot went very low. Low meant below the height of the tree lines. The pilot approached tree line after tree line fast and low only to pop up sharply at the last minute and drop equally sharply on the other side. I saw it as an "E" ticket ride at Disneyland in 1968. To his credit, the new FO took it well, if with a touch of green in his complexion.

Refining My "Land Navigation" Skills

Once on the ground in our new AO, the company commander (CO) told me to show our new FO what we did on a patrol. He instructed me to take my platoon to the western edge of our AO. This is a completely flat area, which is what you get when the terrain is mostly underwater year-round. In this abandoned area, we found occasional small, widely scattered areas of solid ground.

A bigger problem arose when I discovered the usual methods to determine one's position on a map were ineffective. The area included no hills or other prominent terrain features on those miles of flat marshes and rice paddies in any direction. I knew my location, but only approximately. Not knowing my exact location is dangerous especially when calling for defensive fire from artillery and mortars, helicopter gunships, or air support.

I remembered a method taught in the artillery portion of OCS. I asked the FO to call for two airbursts with white smoke. You take compass bearings from the two airbursts and draw them on the map. Where they intersect is your location on the map with an excellent degree of precision.

It did not quite work as planned. I got the fragments from one of the airbursts. Ducking the trash prevented me getting a compass bearing. I checked on my men. No one got hurt.

I saw we stood directly in line with the trajectory of the shell. The artillery did not know my location and I did not know its location. To call in defensive fire, I give map coordinates and an azimuth to the target. The artillery then knows generally where I am when setting up the shot. This avoids the problem except when calling for close support. In such a situation, my problems at hand are shooting at us, making close support a necessity not an option.

I told the FO to move the airburst a thousand meters to a third intersection of grid lines. The battery needed definitive authorization from the field commander for a third shot. The artillery wanted my initials. To use my initials violates operational security rules. Some rules I did obey. I told the FO to give the battery my radio call sign, Hostile Pistol 1 6 (phonetically "one six"). The battery was satisfied.

The battery fired the airburst. I got my second bearing. With the two bearings, I established my location to within one hundred meters, the accuracy expected of a platoon leader. I was ready to call in supporting artillery or mortar fire if required.

Hostile Pistol was the radio call sign for D Company; 1 meant 1st Platoon and 6 meant the platoon leader. These changed monthly except for the numbers.

I learned an important lesson when I started to lead my platoon on patrols. The training we received in OCS first introduced us to the combat leadership skills we needed to develop, but in a piecemeal fashion. Later training honed those skills. The reality of war is I might find myself in situations where I employed these skills in various combinations or all at the same time. Better to learn it now.

One primary skill is to know exactly where my men and I are located on the map at all times. We call it land navigation. Whether I needed help, or I needed to help another platoon or I needed to reach an objective, the initial fact upon which to base my actions was my location on the map. I checked my location at irregular intervals. In open country, the intervals were longer, maybe every fifteen to twenty minutes. In the swamps, jungles and mountains with limited view of landmarks or of lack of landmarks, I checked my compass heading and the maps every ten to fifteen minutes.

This became instinctive when on the move. My proficiency continued to improve. I relied on my ability to read the map and compare what it depicted to what I was seeing in front of me. Essentially, I was learning to transform a two-dimensional map into a 3D picture in my head. Later I developed an ability to memorize the terrain of my route. I only used my compass to keep me headed in the right direction.

How I Lost My Radio Telephone Operator

I experienced an incident shortly after D Company started patrolling its new AO. It took place on resupply day. The company came together for every resupply. Each of my men was busy with storing the new C-rations and other items he had received. Some were changing into clean jungle fatigues, underwear and socks so they could turn in their dirty ones for washing. Others read their letters from home which came with the resupply. Everything proceeded smoothly.

A sergeant from another platoon came to my platoon's location. I didn't know of his presence until I heard a disturbance not far from me. I turned around to see him and "JJ," my Radio Telephone Operator (RTO), fighting. I saw JJ strike this sergeant. It took place in full view of my platoon. They also saw that I witnessed JJ strike the sergeant.

JJ, a private first class, just struck a Non-Commissioned Officer (NCO). That is a prison offense. Pretending I hadn't seen it and leaving the matter to my platoon sergeant, the traditional solution to avoid a court-martial, was out of the question. The fight stopped when I approached them to investigate what had happened.

The sergeant had brought a bottle of cheap whiskey and shared it with JJ. As a result, both became intoxicated. JJ, not much of a drinker, was the worse of the two. The sergeant was not a seasoned NCO; he was a recent graduate of the Army's new ninety-day Non-commissioned Officer Candidate School. This kind of incident rarely happens with experienced NCOs.

Yes, I know Officer Candidate School is only twice as long but the extra time makes all the difference in developing leadership skills. The sergeant deliberately did or said something to JJ. Whatever it was, it triggered JJ's alcohol-fired anger. Still, that is no justification for him striking an NCO, but it is mitigating.

I reported the incident to my company commander. I made it clear JJ was a good soldier and RTO. I added I didn't want him severely punished because the sergeant set things in motion when he got JJ drunk. I finished by saying I wanted to keep JJ as my RTO. I don't think my CO was happy about the problem or about my bringing it to him or asking for leniency for JJ. He took no official action against JJ except to transfer him out of the company, which satisfied me. JJ didn't get a black mark on his record or a prison sentence from a court-martial.

Before I reported the incident to my commander, I had a quiet one-sided talk with the sergeant. His misbehavior, cavalier attitude, and the loss of my RTO angered me. It showed. I led him far enough away to avoid any of the lower ranking soldiers overhearing what I said to him. I did not want to risk impairing his authority as a sergeant or making him a laughing stock.

My anger gave me a sharp tone of voice. I ordered him to stand at attention. This shocked him. I told him he created the situation. In plain language, I told him to stay out of my platoon's area unless he came on official business or I'd kill him. I told him to get out. I think he believed me. Fortunately, D Company's platoons rarely operated together. I kept this matter between us and did not report him to his platoon leader. I do not recall ever seeing him again.

Contingency Planning

Contingency planning became another aspect of knowing my location. I used my growing skill to interpret the map to locate any points that lent themselves to our ambushes, or to see where the enemy might ambush us. The flat terrain of the rice paddies coupled with the lack of significant foliage explained the scarcity of ambush sites. After two or three months, I became familiar, to the point of boredom, with our AO. I didn't often need the map for navigation unless a firefight started elsewhere in D Company's AO.

A critical skill is visualizing the terrain depicted on the map so I could see what terrain features were likely ambush sites for the Viet Cong or us. The problem with an ambush is the men are not well positioned for defense against an attack from the rear or the side. Having my squads, roughly seven to nine men each, well dispersed in the open terrain offered me the possibility of maneuvering the squads not caught in the ambush against an attacker's flanks or rear.

My standing order had two parts: (1) the squad or squads caught in the ambush would immediately return maximum fire by firing two magazines on fully automatic to suppress the enemy's fire, and (2) follow up with an assault on the ambush yelling and screaming like maniacs while keeping their rate of fire as high as possible. The squads not caught in the ambush would move to assault its flanks or rear as I directed.

The point was to move rapidly. You can get killed if you stay in an ambush's kill zone.

An unexpected and violent counterattack may defeat an ambush, thereby reducing our casualties and increasing the enemy's. This became my basic plan, not forgetting "no plan survives contact with the enemy" (Prussian Field Marshal l Karl Graf von Moltke). Flexibility was always a key factor in my planning lest they go awry.

A firefight is cacophony personified, filled with noise, confusion, screaming and gunfire. In the midst of all that commotion, I needed to maneuver my rifle squads to overcome the enemy, accomplish my mission, adjust supporting artillery fires, coordinate ground attacks by helicopters and fixed wing aircraft, keep track of the number of my men still able to fight, making sure my Medic took care of the wounded, getting helicopter medevacs for my wounded, monitoring the status of our ammunition, keeping my CO apprised of my situation, all the while trying to keep myself alive despite being visible to my men as I went about my job always displaying confidence and competence but never displaying fear.

This was my job. No problem!

Fortunately, we never found ourselves in such a desperate situation which called for all those activities. I found the only way to prepare for combat was to become rather cold and focused on the task at hand, not a perfect solution. But I did find time to practice or review the various aspects of my job. The one exception was coming under fire, a situation over which I controlled only half of the decision.

The Rice Paddies Dry Out by Summer

The rice paddies were small, individual, contiguous plots of land, each approximately forty feet on a side. They surrounded the villages. The divisions between the plots consisted of eighteen-inch high by twelve-inch-wide, flat-topped, packed mud paddy dykes. Over the years, they'd become packed so hard many did not change much from year to year. They usually offered a firm surface for walking.

The paddies filled with water during the rainy season, the time for planting and growing. They were allowed to nearly dry out immediately before the harvest. They stayed dry until the next planting season.

The paddies were dry by the time the locals completed harvesting. My men could take cover behind the paddy dykes dry or when filled with water; dry is better. The tabletop flat land provided an unobstructed view for hundreds of meters in most directions. We could see and be seen across the dry paddies. A wheat field is a good approximation of the hundreds of acres of rice paddies filled with ripe rice stalks.

Most of our days of patrolling were boring and repetitious. We arose quietly before dawn and readied ourselves for an attack. If no attack happened, and there weren't any, we ate breakfast and took care of personal hygiene matters.

I met with my sergeants to discuss what I intended to do for the day. I sought their ideas then and throughout the day, for the simple reason their different perspectives allowed me to see points I missed. My sergeants were good and experienced soldiers whose opinions I valued. But my job was to make the decision.

Combat is different. It does not allow for much discussion. When under fire, there is no time to discuss options. My job is to make instantaneous decisions without input from my sergeants. I gave them orders but left them some flexibility in how they accomplished them. They knew the reality of command and trusted me to not get them killed. I worked constantly to not betray their trust. It is called loyalty. It goes up and down the chain of command. That thought always stayed in the forefront of my thinking. Truly.

Combatting Boredom and Complacency in Patrolling a Featureless Area

The area the first platoon patrolled was large enough that I never saw one of the other platoons in the distance. Its wide-open spaces with a minimal number of trees and high underbrush made for easy patrolling. It did not take long to exhaust the ways to vary our patrolling enough to be interesting or keep us alert. I tried to vary each day's activities to ward off boredom and complacency. However, complacency always lurked. I too got bored. The risks of sniper fire, or ambushes were real. Complacency can get you killed. A change was needed.

We usually broke for the lunch meal around noon if we held a defensible position. I met with my sergeants again to discuss what I intended for the afternoon. A key goal of the afternoon was to locate ambush sites with the promise of interdicting enemy movements at night. Hope springs eternal. We returned to patrolling after lunch. One objective was to identify the ambush sites for the coming night. A great difficulty was the lack of ambush sites good or bad. There were not many in our AO.

We typically broke for the evening meal around dusk. My sergeants and I met again to discuss my plans for positioning the squads for ambushes. In the waning moments of sunlight, I sent the sergeants and their squads to their ambush sites. I accompanied a different squad each night.

The men in each ambush took turns alternating between sleeping and watching throughout the night. It was not ideal but it provided them with enough rest while making an effective ambush. Just before dawn, we readied ourselves for an attack. If there was no attack, we started the next day in the same fashion.

We patrolled the AO without any enemy activity for several months, during which time I was promoted to first lieutenant. A first lieutenant's insignia of rank is a silver bar. The Army adopted subdued rank insignia for use in Vietnam. A first lieutenant's insignia of rank became a black bar. Our Parachutist Badges (silver winged parachutes) followed a similar scheme.

I elected to wear the white bar on my collar and helmet, with a white Parachutist Badge above the white bar on the helmet rather than the subdued versions. Some questioned this practice, thinking I set myself up for an enemy sniper. Perhaps, but think about this: I usually walked with a map or a compass in my hand. An RTO with a radio and whip antenna on his back followed me everywhere like a shadow. I doubted the black insignia ever fooled a sniper. A bit of *bravado* is needed sometimes.

Field Rations Lacked Variety but We Found Solutions to Add Some

Early on, we came across a partially destroyed and abandoned cement block home. Sometime in the past, the owners planted a small vegetable garden. It grew wild after they left. The only vegetables interesting to us were the scallions, which enhanced the taste of our C-rations.

The scallions really were an important find in terms of taste. They helped keep morale up. A case of C-rations contains twelve different meals of which only one was a breakfast. Each case contained the same twelve meals as every other case in its production lot. Those production lots were years long, sometimes a decade or more. Most of the meals were okay, but it does not take long before boredom

Resupply by UH-1 helicopter, D Company in the rice paddies west of Saigon, 1968.

sets in. Imagine eating the same twelve meals week after week for a year.

Anything to break the dining monotony was a good thing. Later, we came across small hot peppers growing wild. We found a way to buy small French bread loaves off the Vietnamese economy. Now we added sandwiches to our diet. Some enterprising infantryman came up with a cookbook for getting more out of our C-rations. I saw a copy once. It contained dozens of recipes.

Our C-rations began to taste much better with the addition of the scallions, peppers and the rolls. We received hot meals every third day during our resupply. They were well received but they only came every third day. The additional flavors we found made daily dining on C-rations more varied and interesting. I could see the men displayed a slightly better humor. Gauging morale is more art than science.

UH-1 helicopter along the Saigon River, south of Saigon and north of the mudflats, 1968.

I Get Blood Poisoning in My Left Arm
but Can't Leave the Field

Sometime in this period, I received an insect bite or a scratch on my lower left forearm. I never knew which but I believe it was an insect. It became infected. The infection began working its way up my arm like blood poisoning. My major symptoms were increasing pain, a high and rising fever and swelling so great my wrist got close to the size my forearm had been before it too began swelling. But the intense pain became my immediate problem.

The pain reached the point where my left arm became virtually useless. Merely bumping it caused excruciating pain. Merely flexing it hurt. The arm got so bad I needed my men to help me put on and take off my rucksack and get me up from a sitting position. I had no doubt I was a liability if we got into a firefight. I could still shoot but rapid reloading takes two functioning arms.

My temperature rose to a tiny fraction under 101 degrees Fahrenheit and threatened to go higher. I experienced occasional brief moments of lightheadedness. My medic could do nothing for me; he had turned in all his antibiotics, prescription strength ointments and morphine because somewhere a few medics had sold theirs on the black market. Everybody else suffered as a result of their greed and selfishness.

A medical evacuation was out of the question. Brigade policy forbade it until one's temperature rose to 101 degrees or above. My temperature held at 100.9 degrees. I failed to qualify for medical evacuation to the rear. I understood the policy targeted malingerers but I had been this way for nearly a week and daily grew worse. But I never asked anything of my men I wouldn't do myself. I stayed in the field. Curiously, if one of my men suffered with the same condition, I'd have ordered his immediate medical evacuation.

D Company returned to the rear for a couple of days rest at the end of the week. Before I saw the battalion's physician, I needed to attend the company officers meeting with our CO for debriefing. This was not a formal affair but a chance for he and his officers to compare notes and observations. We drank a beer or two during the informal debriefing.

Once the debriefing was finished the company commander sent me to the battalion doctor. He examined me, questioned me and took my temperature. I do not recall his diagnosis but I received two huge shots of an antibiotic, one in each posterior cheek. I was a bit foggy at the time but I think I heard him order six million units of whatever he shot into each cheek.

He gave me a muscle relaxer also. It worked wonders once it reached the alcohol from the beer. I felt like I was floating as I made my way to the cot assigned to me in another tent with a sand floor. I don't know how I found the correct tent or cot. The combination of the alcohol and the muscle relaxer had taken effect pretty quickly.

Much of what little I remember after the shots has always been a blur. I barely reached the cot in time. All I remember is dropping onto the cot as unconsciousness closed in. I awoke in the morning to find the pain nearly gone, the swelling in my arm down, and my temperature had broken. I was fit for duty by the following day. What I went through in those days was worse than the illness which nearly got me killed a few months earlier on the convoy to Da Nang but only because of its longer duration.

I picked up more serious infections in my first eight months in Vietnam than I did in the rest of my life with one exception. I contracted acute interstitial pneumonia in 2018. It too came close to killing me.

An Unexploded Artillery Shell

I usually walked near the head of the platoon or squad if we were spread out as we patrolled. The importance of this became apparent one day when we passed by an unexploded 105 mm artillery shell, a powerful piece of ordnance. A 105 mm artillery shell has a bursting (lethal) radius of fifty meters (one hundred sixty-four feet). I told my platoon sergeant to move the platoon two hundred meters away and get behind something for protection. I took no chances my men could be injured. I intended to destroy it in place lest the Viet Cong use it against us with devastating effect, either as a command-detonated mine or a booby trap.

I kept a lock of C-4 plastic explosive (a pound and a quarter) in my rucksack. I used the adhesive on the back of the block to attach it to the shell. I primed it with the electric blasting cap from my Claymore mine. The farthest I could get from the shell was one hundred feet which is the length of the Claymore Mine's electric cord I intended to use to detonate the shell.

My RTO and I took cover behind an exceptionally large and robust three-foot-high paddy dyke. I shouted "Fire in the hole" a couple of times to let my men know it was time to get down behind a paddy dyke. I squeezed the hand-held electric generator to detonate the C-4 and the artillery shell.

It worked perfectly. The C-4 detonated the shell with an explosion much louder than I expected, the loudest explosion I ever heard because of the proximity of it. I think I used too much C-4. Fortunately, my RTO and I were uninjured. Later I heard the blast was so loud my men thought I'd blown myself up. When I related this story to my family, they used the word crazy.

My Company Commander Gets Sniped At

Late one night, I heard a few shots from an AK-47 (they're distinctive) in the distance. I heard no return fire. My CO radioed me about a sniper firing at his command group. He added no one was wounded. In the next breath, he told me to send a squad to his location to look for the sniper. I think his command group and the mortar crew consisted of only six or seven men counting him.

I told him "Yes sir," fully intending to get my men moving. I added my concern about the possibility of a trap to draw one of the platoons into the open and ambush it. We both knew the Viet Cong frequently used that all too familiar tactic.

I also reminded him it was the dry season with dry paddies empty of rice plants and we had a bright moon. My men would be visible from a great distance while crossing nearly a kilometer of moonlit, open, flat ground to reach him. He agreed with my assessment and cancelled his order. I told him should he need us, *we would be there*!

I keep my promises. I would have led most of my platoon to the company command post and left a squad to protect the rucksacks and bedding we would leave behind. Travelling at a fast trot is easier without the weight of the rucksacks. With the rucksacks, running is more like lumbering. We could be moving in less than five minutes, arriving between ten and fifteen minutes later.

If we were ambushed, I intended for us to attack the ambush force by running directly at and through it. Would the shock of our attacking from a run cause the VC to break and run? I'll never know. But it did work for the Greeks at the Battle of Marathon. (I read a lot.)

I cannot speak for anyone else, but the unwritten rule among those of us who do the actual fighting is if one of our units needs help in a desperate situation, they get it. Period! Any necessary questions get asked after the situation is resolved. We will fight our way to them if necessary, and keep attacking until we reach them, much as General Patton did in the Third Army's relentless drive to relieve the 101st Airborne Division at Bastogne.

Infantrymen follow their officers into combat, not because they were ordered to do so, but because they know we will not abandon or desert them. They know they will see us leading every attack from a position in front of them, not from behind them. The motto for Infantry OCS is "Follow Me." It was on the shoulder patches we wore.

If I refused to go to the command group's assistance when it was under fire, aside from the court-martial, I would lose the confidence and respect of my men. They would be reluctant to follow me into combat, and rightly so. That could spell disaster in a firefight. "Rank hath its privileges." It also has its honor and tradition-bound obligations.

We would kill the sniper immediately upon our arrival, unless he instantly surrendered. I would bring my interpreter to translate his sole option to him.

I'm Bulletproof?

One late afternoon, as twilight began, we finished our evening meals and waited for darkness to fall over the area before moving to our night ambush positions. I waited sitting cross-legged on uneven ground when I heard small arms fire a considerable distance from us. A split second later, a bullet struck my upper left arm and knocked me over. Thinking I'd been shot, I called to my medic seated a couple of meters away.

He started to laugh; I think he thought I was joking. I checked myself for injuries and found none. The only evidence of my being struck by a bullet was a small tear in my left shirtsleeve.

Near the end of twilight, I started to roll down the left sleeve when a spent bullet tumbled out. Imagine my twofold surprise at seeing the bullet and realizing how close I had come to earning a Purple Heart Medal. The bullet fell into the tall grass. I couldn't use my flashlight to find it because showing light at night invites trouble. I really wanted the bullet as a souvenir but I made no further attempts to find it.

A Visit from the Brigade Commander Improves My Relationship with My CO

D Company received orders to participate in a Cordon and Search operation in the largest village in our AO. We were the cordon; a team of South Vietnamese soldiers did the searching.

The 1st Platoon received orders to cordon off the one kilometer along the west side of the village. I was down to about thirty-five men by this time. The reasons were sickness or other noncombat related issues. The risk to each paratrooper was too great to string them out individually. Instead, I placed them in two- and three-man strongpoints spaced about 100 meters apart for mutual support.

This village was blessed with a large shade tree centered on its western side. It afforded a shaded view of the entire west side of the village out to four or five hundred meters. Logic and tactics said I should set up my command post there. Shade from large trees is a rare sight in the rice growing areas in South Vietnam.

Periodically, I went up and down the line of my men to make sure they were doing okay, check their water needs, and touch bases with my sergeants.

I stood in the shade leaning on the tree when my radio operator told me our CO wanted us to mark a landing zone for the brigade commander's helicopter. I gave a smoke grenade to my medic, told him where I wanted him to throw it and went back to leaning on the tree. The smoke grenade landed about a hundred feet from my command post.

I sent runners to alert the men that the brigade commander was coming. I returned to casually leaning against the tree. By casual, I mean my sleeves and pants legs were rolled up because of the heat. I had set down my rucksack. I wore my loadbearing harness and the bandoliers of loaded M-16 magazines. My M-16 rested against the tree trunk in reach if I needed it.

One must be fashionable, even in combat. Below the front edge of my steel helmet, I wore a pair of French wraparound sunglasses made famous by Jean-Claude Killy, the French Olympic skier in the early 1960s. I do not remember where I lost them or how.

I watched the helicopter set down. At the same time, I caught sight of my CO rounding the corner of a nearby thatched hut. I picked up my rifle and watched him. His steel helmet sort of bobbled on his head as he tried to run while getting his loadbearing harness on properly. Accouterments in order, he met and exchanged salutes with the brigade commander once he alighted from the helicopter. They walked towards me because my tree offered the only shade from the scorching sun.

For the point of this part of the story to hold any meaning, the reader needs to know my CO and I had gotten off on the wrong foot days before I was assigned to his company. It was just one of those things and nothing of any importance. But I knew it still annoyed him.

As the brigade commander and my CO reached the point where saluting was appropriate, I stood to attention, rendered a proper salute and greeted them formally. Instead of returning my salute, Colonel Bolling held out his hand for a handshake saying, "Hi Mike, want to come back and work for me again?" My CO's eyes seemed to grow wider. I believe he thought I was another inexperienced replacement. He didn't know I once served as one of Colonel Bolling's special staff officers.

I politely declined the offer, truthfully added I liked where I was. My relationship with my CO became better. More proof it is good to have friends in high places. I still didn't abuse it. I commanded a rifle platoon. I needed nothing more.

The days in this AO dragged on with little new to keep the mind alert. We got those two-quart bladders around this time. Each of us carried more drinkable water with him from that day forward. While technically an important change, boredom and complacency became more and more difficult to ward off. I did everything I could think of to change our daily activities. How do you inject change into a situation every aspect of which you have explored multiple times? None of us knew it but a change approached.

6

Pineapples and a Missing Battalion Commander

December 1968 to 20 March 1969

A Reconnaissance in Force into the Pineapple Plantation

D Company got the mission to conduct a reconnaissance in force of the pineapple plantation a handful of kilometers southwest of Saigon. It had been long known as a VC bastion and a tough nut to crack. Our orders charged us to engage any Viet Cong forces remaining there. This is military language to kill or capture any VC we encountered, which made it a classic search and destroy mission.

While the plantation lay in the Capital Military District, our distance from it dictated an air assault. Helicopters would drop us off about a hundred meters from the edge of the pineapple plantation. Water covered the landing zone. My orders required the 1st Platoon to advance through waist-deep water toward a tree line from which the Viet Cong could shoot at us from dry or semi-dry land. Our pre-mission briefing on the enemy situation omitted the high water but told us to expect resistance.

The UH-1 helicopters hovered about four to five feet above the water to let us jump in. I thought about the lack of buoyancy in the eighty pounds of weapons, and related gear each of us carried. I wonder if my men had similar thoughts before they jumped.

The tips of densely packed reeds projected four to six inches above the water's surface. The only way to tell the depth of the water around them was to jump from the helicopters. I didn't hesitate and jumped first.

Two good facts became obvious when I hit the water. One, the water did not rise above my waist and no one shot at us.

We accomplished the air assault without receiving any enemy fire, which means absolutely nothing. The enemy could wait for our helicopters to leave us stranded in high water and dense reeds. Stranded is the correct term because the combination of water and reeds prevented us from moving rapidly. This problem also never appeared in the briefing. No one makes good time wading through water that deep, especially if you're weighed down with the upwards of eighty pounds of gear we carried. Then came the second problem.

I tried to walk but the reeds grew so close together moving through them was difficult. The reeds caught and trapped one of my feet but my upper body, overbalanced by my heavy rucksack, continued forward. I fell and discovered the reeds, despite being densely packed, failed to support me when I put my hands down to stop my fall. I continued falling forward into the water. The reeds did slow my fall.

I watched the water level slowly rise up in the lenses of my sunglasses while I sank. How bizarre I thought, to drown during an air assault by helicopter. At last, I got my feet under me and stood up. On such a hot day, my dip into the cool water felt quite refreshing.

The enemy didn't open fire on us while we waded toward the tree line despite a total lack of anything to shield us from incoming fire. This must have somewhat resembled what the soldiers and Marines faced on those beach assaults during World War II. Of course, they enjoyed naval gunfire and air support. Did we surprise the Viet Cong was the question in my mind? If so, I doubted their surprise would last much longer.

Next came the *pièce de résistance*. Our pre-mission briefing omitted another critical detail. A UH-1 helicopter flew fast and low along the tree line, my immediate objective. A thick white cloud of smoke billowed from the engine exhaust and trailed behind the helicopter.

My first thoughts were, did the enemy shoot it down? Did my

men and I stand in waist deep water packed with reeds in a hot landing zone with zero concealment and less cover. By hot, I mean under enemy fire. My immediate concern was to get my men moving before we became the target. One odd fact returned after the UH-1 departed; I heard no gunfire from enemy weapons.

I found out later our battalion commander decided, on his own, to use a helicopter to lay down a smoke screen for us. Apparently telling his field commanders this most interesting aspect of our air assault had slipped his mind. I can't print my immediate thoughts about my battalion commander.

D Company rapidly moved through the thinning smoke to the tree line. Having reached the tree lines unopposed, the four platoons of D Company moved into a column formation. The 1st Platoon got the honor of acting as D Company's rearguard, an important military function. My mission as rearguard was to block an enemy's attempt to attack D Company from the rear or to cut it off from reinforcements. We had yet to come under enemy fire.

Once we moved beyond the tree line, we saw where the pineapples grew. Row upon row of berms shaped like long pyramids greeted us. Despite the overgrowth on the mounds, I saw the occasional small pineapple growing on them. I grabbed one in passing. It did not taste bad but was too small and prickly for casual eating. Fortunately, none of the VC shot at us.

We advanced deeper into the plantation without drawing enemy fire. Soon we came across signs the Air Force and artillery had worked it over on more than one occasion. I saw innumerable bomb and shell craters of varying sizes. The water in the larger older craters tended to be clear with bright colors. The colors came from the chemical residue of the bombs and shells. It said, in no uncertain terms, the water was poisoned and utterly undrinkable. The water in the newer and smaller craters was opaque and mud colored, which reminded me of the Mississippi River.

The plantation had internal tightly packed raised earth roads. I estimated them at five feet wide, enough to drive a water buffalo pulling a cart or a jeep along them.

The ones I saw were lined with fighting positions dug into their edges. The positions resembled rectangular foxholes, each large enough to allow two or three VC to fight easily from them. They gave good protection from our return fire and supporting artillery fires.

The VC staggered the holes alternating from one side of the road to the other. Five meters separated the holes along each edge of the road. What a daunting thing to see, more daunting if we fought to take it or to move along it. Especially because we still stood in waist deep water.

My company commander gave me orders to proceed to a certain set of map coordinates while the company continued its advance. They would catch up the following day. My men and I left the plantation's roads and struck off to the coordinates. We had not seen a single Viet Cong soldier or evidence of their recent presence in the plantation.

The terrain in the direction of our new destination was under only ankle-deep water the color of the mud and impossible to see through. This presented a new danger to my men.

We no longer saw where the smaller bomb and shell craters lay. The large bombs took out a large swath of the plant life and left an area bare of any plants. The small bombs, shells, and rockets did this too but their telltale signs resembled naturally occurring gaps in the scraggly ground cover.

We slogged along until suddenly I saw the man ahead of me sink out of sight. He'd stepped into one of those hidden shell craters. All that remained of him was his steel helmet floating upside down. The fact he didn't immediately reappear meant his heavy rucksack held him under water and possibly drowning.

I knew the crater couldn't be deep. I felt for the edge of the crater with my foot. When I found it, I simultaneously reached into the water near the helmet and felt around for him. My hand struck the metal frame of his rucksack. I grabbed the frame and pulled him up. He was no worse for the experience, except for being soaking wet. But on this hot day, I knew from recent experience a brief dip is refreshing.

Sometime earlier, I'd received a Kit Carson Scout to assist me. A former member of the Viet Cong in the area near Saigon, he had

1st Platoon, D Company, disembarking a Navy landing craft at a village south of Saigon, 1968.

come over to our side under an amnesty program. He was only sixteen years old. I learned his Scout pay allowed him to buy a small motorcycle, which improved his chances with the young ladies in Saigon. This and our talks made me think he favored no political ideology.

His presence enhanced my ability to perform my missions in two ways. It allowed me to converse with the Vietnamese people I met. My pitiful few words of Vietnamese failed miserably. This offered the promise of advance warning of enemy activity in the area, particularly if the information concerned a planned attack on my platoon or the company.

It also gave me the opportunity to speak, more like chitchat, with the Vietnamese who lived in our AO. This chitchat improved our relations with the people and helped us gain their trust, always an important consideration.

His other capability showed its value during our march from the pineapple plantation. He showed me how to spot the hidden small bomb or shell craters including where to walk to avoid stepping into them. I passed this useful tip along to my men. Since we'd already departed the company, passing it to them had to wait until the company caught up with us.

While this capability didn't win the war, it kept more of my men away from the risk of drowning in an unseen bomb or shell crater.

I led my men toward the map coordinates my company commander gave me. We left the pineapple plantation and now strode through progressively thicker, interwoven vegetation consisting of large bushes, small trees and vines until darkness fell. Then we broke through into an area of nearly impassable vegetation.

Once we struggled through it, we immediately came to a small canal about two meters wide with another wall of thicker vegetation on the far side. We entered the chest deep water of the canal and crossed it.

Standing in chest deep water while struggling to get through the far side vegetation made the job harder. We fought our way through thick vegetation to find ourselves on dry ground again.

I notified my company commander I had reached the map coordinates. He told me to wait for new orders in the morning and to stay put. I set the men up in a defensive perimeter on our small oasis of *terra firma*. The canal overgrown with the thick vegetation to our rear made an excellent barrier. Our recent experience told me I would hear anyone trying to cross the canal. I used one squad to cover our rear. Better safe than sorry.

I placed two of my squads and both of my M-60 machine guns in a semi-circle behind the paddy dyke arc facing the rice paddies to our front. The tall rice was nearly ready for harvesting. It looked much like the wheat fields I remembered seeing as a young boy on a small farm in the Midwest. I located my command group—my platoon sergeant, our RTOs, my medic, the scout, and me in the middle.

The early morning arrived with no untoward events during the night. I awaited orders from my CO. While I enjoyed the early morning sun and drying out, I drank a cup of hot chocolate. One of my machine gunners ran up to me, breaking this moment of tranquility. In his excitement, he repeatedly said, "Sir, you have to come see this."

I responded, "What is it?"

He responded with the same phrase. We went back and forth like this a couple of times before it became obvious, he wanted me to see his mysterious something and wouldn't stop until I did.

He took me to his machine gun. It straddled the twelve-inch paddy dyke where I ordered its emplacement when we arrived last night. Finally, I got to see why he was excited.

One unexploded Chinese anti-personnel mine with the safety pin gone lay directly under the machine gun's barrel on the far side of the paddy dyke! I said with a note of disbelief, "What's wrong with you? Why didn't you tell me about this back there? I would've believed you."

Carefully, I removed the gun from the paddy dyke and gave it to the gunner. Next, I ordered the nearby men to move away from the mine. I instructed my sergeants to make sure everybody knew about the mine and its location and my orders to stay away from it. When we left, I blew it up with a hand grenade. I learned my lesson about too much explosive with the 105 mm shell.

While waiting there, we received a box of something by helicopter. It contained things like today's power bars, granola bars, and pemmican bars. The foodstuffs tasted good, anything different from our usual fare is always a good thing. Except for one problem, not enough to go around. I told my sergeants divide them as evenly as possible among the men.

I have forgotten everything else it contained except a battery powered strobe light for marking our position at night. When turned on, the strobe pulsed a rhythmic bright white light easily seen for thousands of meters at night. To an aircraft crew in flight, it would look exactly like muzzle flashes from weapons firing up at them. No way would I ever use it to mark my position for any type of aircraft carrying machine guns, rockets, or bombs. I kept it, just in case, but never used it.

Late in the afternoon, the rest of D Company finally came out of the pineapple plantation a hundred meters from us. I received orders to rejoin them. With the arrival of twilight, we moved out and set up a company size ambush in the rice paddies, one of the rare times the four platoons of D Company operated close together.

The darkness of night came with a sense of peace. We enjoyed a light cool breeze. The ambient light came from a beautiful starry sky. The night's tranquility disappeared the instant a machine gunner in one of the other platoons opened fire on something he saw outside his perimeter. He fired burst after burst into his target, apparently to no effect, except for ricochets going in many directions, hence the repeated firing. Finally, someone who saw the gunner's target said he hit his target and killed it. The shooting and the ricocheting tracers stopped.

Of course, everyone within a two-mile radius now knew our position. Come the dawn, we all saw he'd shot at one of the cement corner posts of a Vietnamese grave. In his defense, I have to add it had a cement ball on top, which, in the dark, would resemble a head. Another tragic case of "Sighted grave, sank same."

A Missing Battalion Commander in a Brothel

We returned to our regular AO after our reconnaissance in force into the pineapple plantation. One of the other rifle companies in our battalion became engaged in a firefight with the VC while we were away. I don't know the details. However, I did hear nobody could locate the battalion commander during the firefight. It turns out he was in a brothel in Saigon. The brigade commander relieved him of his command. The change of command ceremony took place the next morning without the usual frills and behind a tent.

7

Mudflats, Ice Cream
and a Man Drowned

1 September 1968 to 30 October 1968

The Mud Flats East of the Rung Sat Special Zone

D Company received another questionable honor. Our mission charged us with conducting a search and destroy operation in an area of uniformly level mud flats, various sized canals, water and more mud.

We planned to hunt for any Viet Cong in an area directly west of the Rung Sat Special Zone but physically separated from it by a branch of a river. The Rung Sat is a large mangrove swamp south of Saigon. Navy Seal teams performed yeoman work in the Rung Sat. I suppose someone decided a company of Army paratroopers was the perfect unit to check out the area west of it. Lucky us.

We received additional maps for this operation. We carried the usual 1:50,000 scale topographic map showing the topography with gridlines. With a little training, you can locate your position on it to within one hundred meters. The elevation lines gave a detailed picture of the terrain features. If you read and understand them, you could form a mental picture of the terrain except in uniformly level mudflats.

The new maps were 1:25,000 scale Picto-Supplement maps. They are blow-ups of aerial color photographs of the terrain. The cameras may have been equipped with flat lenses to avoid the distortion a more rounded lens gives to the edge of the photograph. This allowed

Photo of the U.S. Embassy in Saigon, taken when I got my passport, July 1969.

the use of a larger scale. They bore the same grid lines as the topographic maps. No matter which of the maps you used, the coordinates were the same.

The Picto-Supplement maps showed the actual canals and vegetation in the area the map covered. It displayed tiny mangrove swamps, some small clumps of Nipa or Nypa Palms, all on a background of otherwise featureless brown mudflats and brown water canals. The two maps together made land navigation much easier and more precise except on the mudflats.

The trouble started immediately after the helicopter landings. A day later, we found out the helicopters landed us nearly a kilometer west of the intended landing zone. Ordinarily, I can quickly determine my exact location. But land navigation on endless mudflats with only the occasional small clump of Nipa palms or the tiny mangrove swamps proved difficult. It's especially hard if your starting point is off by a kilometer.

My orders said take 1st Platoon west to certain map coordinates a kilometer west of our landing site. I studied both maps intently to develop a mental picture of the terrain and vegetation features at my target point and those along the way. I aimed to reach a trail about three or four feet wide, which ran perpendicular to my path. To know when I reached it, I counted my strides until I hit a thousand meters. I knew the length of my stride. It's simple math from there.

I saw a trail of the correct size running in the correct direction exactly where the map showed it to be. Except, I stood on the wrong trail. Ironically, where the helicopters landed us was my objective. By chance the terrain a kilometer away matched what I expected to see.

This is a critical error when calling for artillery fire. I might call them down on my men. I learned an important lesson. The maps may not always display all the terrain features the ground has. We got it straightened out the next day but in the interim, I was what we called "misoriented."

The mudflats, really large plains of mud, contained many small "islands" of mangrove swamps. The smallest I saw was maybe ten meters wide. Clumps of Nipa palms grew randomly in the area. Nipa palms' fronds seemed to grow straight out of the mud. Consequently, I never saw a Nipa palm's trunk.

Canals ranging up to fifty feet across and twenty feet deep laced the mudflats. This opaque, milk chocolate colored water also reminded me of the Mississippi River. Unlike the Mississippi, the canals were uniformly disgusting. Since they ran close to the ocean, they filled and emptied with the ebb and flow of the ocean tides. When the tides changed the garbage from Saigon floated back and forth with the changes.

The true mangrove swamps of the Rung Sat offered a passable picture of Hell on earth. I experienced moments of this Hell in the small mangrove swamps on our side of the river. But they had to be investigated for an enemy's presence. There were none.

The density of the trees in the Rung Sat pointed to a place of heat, humidity and tangled roots, an ugly place to wage war. I respect the SEALs but I wanted no part of the Rung Sat for my men or me. At least on the mudflats, we usually stayed out of the water, if not the mud.

The rise in the water levels of the canals from the rising tides played havoc with our nighttime positions. I set up the platoon's first ambush where two canals joined. I thought I'd picked a place from which we could interdict both. That night the mudflat between the canals flooded when the tide changed. We soon found ourselves in about four inches of water. To avoid the certain onset of total fatigue from patrolling all day and ambushing by night, I usually had the men sleep in shifts during the ambushes, but you don't sleep well lying in four inches of water. I spent the night sitting on a tree stump where I tried to get some sleep. None of us got much sleep. On the other hand, our situation came with a silver lining of a sort; all of us were alert and rather pissed off. Any enemy watercraft passing us was doomed. None did.

The mud on the sides and bottom of the canals was scary. Its color and consistency was similar to milk chocolate pudding. It usually ranged from two to three feet deep. We learned another important lesson; the deep mud of the canal sides trapped anyone who stepped into it. The grip of this mud could dislocate a man's hip while we pulled him free of it. Consequently, crossing them was a lengthy and dangerous proposition at any time. To try when under fire would be tantamount to suicide.

Some days later, we came across another of the small canals we needed to cross. The daylight gave me the opportunity to examine the crossing problem and surrounding area. We needed a way to cross without getting stuck in the mud while avoiding potential slaughter if the Viet Cong caught us trapped and exposed.

I looked around to see if nature provided anything to help. After a few more minutes of thought, I remembered a fragment of something I had seen in an old movie or in the Boy Scouts. I decided to modify it a little and see if it helped to cross the canal.

I spread the bulk men out in a defensive posture. I told the men with the few machetes we carried to cut down the fronds of the nearby Nipa Palms and cut them close to the mud. I ordered a few of the others to carry the fronds to the canal.

I showed them what I had in mind. We laid the fronds to cover both sides and the bottom of the canal in several overlapping layers. It took more than two dozen palm fronds. It worked superbly, quickly and on the first try. We'd made a palm frond footbridge strong enough to keep us from sinking into the canal's mud.

Now my men were able to cross the canals at low tide without touching the mud. This method was eminently safer than trying to pull men free from the grip of the canal mud. Its primary use would come when we needed it to cross a small canal while under enemy fire. It gave us a viable option in a combat situation.

A second advantage from building a palm frond footbridge allowed me to use a near maximum amount of my platoon's firepower, which was a lot, to keep the Viet Cong's heads pinned down when my men crossed the canal to assault an enemy force. Being able to construct one quickly would give me the option to lead an assault across the canal. I think seeing my men and I running across the canal on a palm frond footbridge to attack them would be a significant shock to the enemy

When we rejoined the company, I learned one of my company commander's RTOs had become stuck in the canal mud while leaving the landing zone. They had a real problem freeing him without dislocating his hip. Nonetheless they succeeded in freeing him from the mud. But not before a helicopter from brigade approached them and radioed it carried ice cream for the company.

I understand my company commander's language became very colorful at that moment. We'd barely landed. The platoons needed to get clear of the area before we drew rifle or mortar fire from any Viet Cong in the area. Asking to deliver the ice cream was a colossal distraction from our mission.

The following days included the usual operations: searching for signs of the enemy during the day, setting ambushes in the mud during the night. We did not see any Vietnamese on the land around us during the day nor did we see signs they had been in the area. We did see them on variously sized boats in the larger canals and a branch of the river, which cut through the area.

At night we totally depended on moon and starlight in the dark. Light amplifying Starlight Scopes were rare on the battlefield. We didn't have one. We only saw a few dozen yards by starlight, less with any cloud cover. The nights with a full moon presented us with a two-edged sword. We saw greater distances, but so did the VC.

One of my squads ambushed a sampan on the river on one of those starlit nights. It came within a few meters of the river's edge. Significantly, it moved against the current when my men sighted it. The people in the area complied with the curfew and the total restriction on using their boats at night. Anyone using such craft at night identified himself as VC. My men opened fire on the boat.

After the shooting, it drifted back on the current in the direction from which it came and out of sight. We never determined how many Viet Cong were in the sampan or what cargo it carried. This turned out to be the extent of actual combat for the D Company during the entire time we operated across from the Rung Sat. Worse, it was the only contact D Company had with the enemy while I served in it. My men did get credit for one enemy killed in action (KIA) because the boat was traveling against the current.

One day we found some unoccupied Viet Cong fortifications. I reported this to my CO. He responded with orders to destroy them. I set out pickets to warn us of the approach of anyone. I had the remainder of my men take turns between destroying the fortifications and guarding our position.

The fortifications consisted of a handful of bunkers. Each was constructed of small diameter logs partially dug into the mud. Their vertical log walls kept their shapes with minimal reinforcement. All were empty except for one with a snake in it. I think it was a large viper. It was not important enough for my men or me to go in to root it out. My men very carefully destroyed the bunker, snake included.

Another Visit from the Brigade Commander

I received orders to mark a landing zone for what turned out to be a command helicopter. This one belonged to Brigadier General Bolling, our recently promoted brigade commander. He and his operations officer wanted to inspect our destruction of the Viet Cong fortifications. The general also landed to see my men at work and talk with them.

After our greetings, no salutes because the chance snipers might see us was ever present, the general asked me to accompany him on a walk around the bunkers. I stood back to take myself out of the picture when he went to talk with my men. He gave no thought to what the mud did to his clean jungle fatigues and shined jungle boots. He acted no different than every man in my platoon, from the lowest ranking private to me. He spoke with the men, asking what they were doing and how they were getting along.

His manner showed he was actually concerned about them and their activities. This concern earned him the respect and loyalty of virtually every man in the brigade including the new replacements. In the process, he got a good look at his soldiers (his only while he was with us) digging in the mud to destroy enemy fortifications.

They and their jungle fatigues were covered in mud. We spent so much time digging in the mud, sitting on it or lying on it, that the color of our jungle fatigues had changed from green to mudflat brown. But their good humor demonstrated their high morale. I have not a scintilla of doubt he felt as proud of those paratroopers as I did.

The General's Operation Officer had issues. He was visibly unhappy about the mud. When you consider we'd been patrolling, eating and sleeping in a uniformly wet, muddy environment, I thought the operation officer's attempt to keep out of the mud was ridiculous.

Before he left, General Bolling asked how things fared with us and if we needed anything. I told him the truth as always; we fared well and needed nothing. He had watched these men all working with a will and a good humor. He knew if they needed anything critical, he would have seen them in a different mood or heard them complaining. I like to think he gave me some credit for their good morale but I will never know.

The general used my radio to speak with my company commander. I stepped aside to give him privacy. I did listen when the topic of ice cream came up. I assumed my CO had tactfully mentioned we couldn't accept the ice cream a day earlier due to the urgency of getting off the landing zone. General Bolling said he would have ice cream sent out in the afternoon. After he left, some of my sergeants and I had a quiet laugh. We knew he would try but we had doubts. Ice cream in the field was a myth.

The Ice Cream Cometh

We were still destroying those well-constructed fortifications two hours later when my RTO caught my attention. I took the handset from him and listened.

I heard a helicopter co-pilot with a brigade call sign on D Company's radio frequency. He called my call sign rather than the company commander's. He requested us to mark our position with a smoke grenade and said he brought ice cream for us. That was a sweet surprise, pun intended. I had a smoke grenade tossed to mark where the general's helicopter had landed earlier.

We received enough chocolate and vanilla ice cream to provide each man with about a quart of one or the other. The more creative of us chose a little of each. We ate all we could before it melted. It made quite a mess what with all the mud we wore on our persons and fatigues. Being remembered and the ice cream were good in a way I lack words to describe.

My men saw in their brigade commander a leader who did not mind getting dirty alongside them and a leader who keeps his word. American soldiers and Marines have followed leaders like him through tens of thousands of engagements and battles and millions of shots and shells.

Years later, I learned about General (then 1st Lieutenant) Bolling's exploits during the D-Day invasion and afterward. I knew my men would have followed him across that beach and into Hell, not because of the ice cream but because he remembered us and kept his word to us. They knew he would not abandon them even if the battle went wrong. I like to believe my men saw some of the same qualities in me because they followed me into some dangerous situations.

History is filled with stories of leaders of General Bolling's caliber. Those leaders instilled courage and a determination to prevail in their men. Places where the memories of brave men in battle still echo, places like Thermopylae and Bastogne. I am happy fortune made him our brigade commander.

My men received their ice cream first. I like to think he remembered his one-time PIO commanded the 1st Platoon. Maybe the ice cream was his way of thanking me for a job well done as a platoon leader and PIO. I too would have followed him into Hell.

A Drowned Paratrooper

We returned to patrolling the mudflats. I don't know why. The mission remained "search and destroy." We only found more mudflats, Nipas, and the small mangrove swamps but nothing to destroy except those fortifications we'd already destroyed.

I received orders from my CO to patrol a new area defined by encrypted coordinates. When I decrypted the coordinates, I saw they were across a large canal, which would separate us from the rest of the D Company. Perplexed at the surprising change, I decrypted them again with the same result.

I radioed my commander and advised him the coordinates were nowhere near where I had been patrolling. He said, "They're where you told me you were all day." Something was wrong. It never occurred to me someone improperly encrypted the new coordinates. If I used more precision in my words, we'd both have seen the error. It was another lesson learned: be precise in your speech.

I had orders and I possessed the materials needed to cross the canal. The canal was far too wide to use the Nipa palm frond bridge idea, plus the tide was in and the canal was full. I prepared to make a small version of a river crossing. One of my paratroopers volunteered to take the end of the nylon rope across the canal and anchor it there. He'd paddled an air mattress halfway across and abruptly sank out of sight.

I, and some other good swimmers, immediately stripped off our jungle fatigues and boots and jumped into the water to help him. We dove repeatedly but the brown water was still completely opaque. I could barely see my hand a few inches in front of my face while under water. We dove where we saw him disappear until exhausted. None of us could find him. His body surfaced the next day with the change of the tide. He'd floated back to us.

My CO didn't encrypt the coordinates himself. He gave them to his RTO to encrypt and send to me. He didn't check his RTO's encryption. He should have. The RTO erred in his encryption of the numbers. This meant when I decrypted them, which I did several times, I received the incorrect coordinates across the canal.

If I'd encrypted those coordinates in a different system and sent them back to my commander, he'd have seen the error and cancelled his orders. Another platoon leader did this after hearing the radio traffic. This is how the initial mistake came to light.

Our mutual mistakes took the life of one of my best soldiers and a good man. I have not forgotten him or his nickname, Sweet Pea. He always wore his steel helmet backwards making him several decades ahead of men's fashion on wearing baseball style caps.

A Brief Riverine Operation

After another week or so, I received orders to board a U.S. Navy landing craft at the edge of the river upon which my men had killed the Viet Cong in the sampan. It was escorted by two fan boats. It appeared the men of the 1st Platoon would be engaged in a slightly fun Riverine operation before we left the mudflats south of Saigon. We boarded it. The U.S. Navy helmsman pulled away from the shore. He knew where to deliver us. The trip was short.

I recognized one of the reporters from my days in the brigade's Public Information Office sitting atop one of the landing craft's walls. I knew he wanted a story about this operation. We talked for a while to get caught up. However, the time for my men and I to disembark stole up on us. I enjoyed those brief moments of reminiscence with him. Seeing him alive, still in one piece and doing well pleased me. I'm sorry we didn't have a story for him.

Street in Saigon near the U.S. Embassy, July 1968.

The Navy landing craft took us to various locations along the river. We disembarked to search for any signs of enemy activity at each of them. We found none. We did find more mud.

I saw some truly huge rats running around on a packed mud ledge under a village built on stilts along the riverbank. The rats were bigger and meatier than a fox terrier. I estimated their size as fifteen inches by twenty inches, not including the tail. They looked to weigh about twenty pounds.

The speed and maneuverability of the fan boats made them ideal for interdicting small boat activity on the river. They darted around and turned on a dime making them fun to ride in too. But we weren't permitted to do that. Navy personnel crewed the landing craft and the fan boats.

We found nothing on land or river. I did take some photographs of the operation in my free moments. This was one of the few times I could do this.

Part One—The 3rd Brigade, 82nd Airborne Division

After another week or so, helicopters came to pick us up. They flew us to the battalion rear area to clean our weapons, our equipment and ourselves. It felt good to be relatively clean once again. Then, we headed back to the rice paddies west of Saigon.

8

Christmas, Bob Hope, a Medcap, and an Airstrike

December 1968

Protecting the Bob Hope Show at Long Binh

The Christmas season found D Company moving to another temporary AO. Long Binh lies about thirty kilometers north of Saigon. It was the headquarters of the U.S. Army in Vietnam. Our mission duplicated the one outside Saigon: prevent any rocket or mortar attacks. The Army needed extra protection around Long Binh because Bob Hope's show would be there.

Once again, we filled our days with patrolling the new AO and setting up ambushes at night. The terrain came with low hills and valleys. Thankfully it contained no rice paddies. Sadly, a significant portion of it was mudflats or muddy.

To cover our AO, our CO scattered the four platoons across it. My portion included the mudflat area in the west. Luckily it was nothing like the endless mudflats and canals west of the Rung Sat Special Zone. We set ambushes in the hope of catching the Viet Cong carrying or setting up their 122 mm rockets or 82 mm mortars. Not one of us saw any of the enemy, let alone had the opportunity to engage them in combat—good for the show and boring for us.

The important point is the Viet Cong launched no rockets or mortar rounds into the show from our AO or anywhere else.

Orders to Hill 15

My platoon and I experienced one notable situation. I received orders to take the 1st Platoon to Hill 15 and occupy it. The number 15 means the top of the hill is 15 meters (48 feet) above sea level. Hill 15 is a small point on the bank of a small river roughly twenty-five meters (27 yards) wide. I saw nothing higher for kilometers on our side of the river. Hill 15 dominated its side of the river. The hills of the far side of the river were easily twenty times as high with denser vegetation and trees.

I received those orders at dusk. We began a 3 kilometer (about 2 mile) march to Hill 15. We slogged through the previously mentioned mudflat. The mud rarely came over the soles of our boots the entire way. When we arrived around nine that night, the men were tired from slogging through the mud. All of us were wet and muddy, again. After thoroughly checking the entire hill for any enemy troops, fortifications and booby traps, we took up night defensive positions on the military crest. The military crest is sufficiently below the real crest to prevent us from being silhouetted against the sky if we stood up.

The monsoon had tapered off; the grasses on the hillsides near the top of this hill were tinder dry due to a lack of recent rain and constant exposure to the sun. The low trees and undergrowth gave us some protection from the sun and some concealment from observation. The hill, while slightly damp and firm to the touch, was drier than the mudflats surrounding it.

I received no information or orders for what was expected of the 1st Platoon on Hill 15. I usually divined what they wanted by looking at the terrain, but I stood on the highest terrain feature on our side of the river; I could see for kilometers in most directions. Maybe we were supposed to interdict enemy traffic on the river. The rest of my suppositions were less plausible than that.

A Mini-Med Cap at Christmas

The river in front of Hill 15 is wide and deep enough for small cargo boats about the size of a family cabin cruiser to navigate. On the morning of the day after we arrived on Hill 15, we saw a cargo boat underway west and upriver. Having no further orders, I flagged it down. A couple of my riflemen, my Medic "Doc," my RTO, my Vietnamese scout/interpreter, and I essentially hitchhiked to get to a nearby village to buy some Coca Colas for those of my men who wanted one.

I motioned for the boat to come to the river shore. This boat was larger than a cabin cruiser. Through my interpreter I learned the Vietnamese family lived on board when it was underway. These were good people and were generous enough to give us a short ride to a nearby village. It wasn't a long ride; the village wasn't more than a kilometer away. We always paid for everything; we did not simply take. We paid for the ride with C-rations, the good meals, not the cast offs.

The wife held an infant clearly in distress. He writhed and cried piteously from pain. Through my interpreter I asked what was wrong. She unwrapped the baby's blanket to show us. The infant had open sores over much of his body. I asked if she would like my medic to examine her baby. She nodded her head rapidly and her eyes sort of lit up at the offer. "Doc" looked at the infant to see how he could help, which wasn't much.

Doc carried the medicinal materials he needed, a few bottles of an antiseptic for cleaning wounds, tubes of Bacitracin (an antibacterial ointment), gauze pads in various sizes and tape. The baby let out some spectacular howls whenever a gauze pad damp with the antiseptic touched his sores. The cleaning could not be avoided; open sores invite infection. Good cleaning was absolutely necessary. Doc moved quickly and as gently as possible.

The ointment Doc applied markedly reduced the baby's pain. He stopped crying almost immediately after Doc applied the ointment. I remember the desperate look on the mother's face replaced with a smile and hope when her baby stopped his crying. He soon fell asleep in her arms. He remained asleep for the rest of our short trip.

Doc gave the mother as much of his antiseptic, Bacitracin ointment, gauze pads and tape as he could spare. Through the interpreter he gave her instructions on how and when to repeat the treatment and to take her child to a doctor as soon as possible.

I read *The Ugly American* around the time I graduated from high school. I remembered the thrust of it. I wanted my men remembered as "Good Americans" not "Ugly Americans." On the occasional times we interacted with the civilian population, we asked for some things and paid if our request was granted. On this boat trip we intended from the start to pay our way.

We left the boat at the town but it was a close call for the boat. The sea was close enough for the rise and fall of the tides to affect the depth of the river. The river was falling; the boat was close to running aground. We sort of organized three or four sampans in the area into a ferry service to take us from the boat to the shore. We paid them too. The cargo boat continued upstream in the nick of time. I never heard what happened to this family or the infant.

We accomplished that rarity in combat, doing something decent in a war zone. We bought the Cokes and walked across the mud flats to Hill 15. The men who wanted a Coke greeted us warmly upon our return. This seemed fitting because the Cokes were warm. We had long ago become accustomed to drinking warm water, Cokes, and beer. This was a very good day.

An Airstrike and a Bomb Damage Assessment

The next day found us still waiting for orders. A flight of two Air Force F-100 fighter-bombers appeared over us about 8 o'clock in the morning. We watched them bomb one of the significantly higher hills on the far side of the river roughly one or two kilometers downriver from us for nearly fifteen minutes.

This wasn't a Hollywood bombing with lots of angst, flames, explosions and secondary explosions, just a slow leisurely attack. We watched it leisurely while eating breakfast. One of the F-100s would make a run, drop a single bomb on the hill, pull up and go around for another attack. The second F-100 repeated the attack in the same fashion. They flew one after the other about two minutes apart until each expended its eight bombs.

This hillside was covered thickly with trees and undergrowth. I couldn't tell the nature of the target, if it'd been hit, or what the damage, if any, the bombs had caused. I didn't see or hear any sign the planes received ground fire. This ruled out the presence of any enemy forces near the point of the bombing. Their bombs expended, they flew away.

We watched the entire attack like a show put on especially for us. We cheered with each bomb's detonation. My men waited through many monotonous days so they greeted any break in the routine with enthusiasm.

Not long after that, my RTO accidently started a fire in the grass around his field expedient stove. This is a small C-ration can with one side pushed in. Put a heat tab in the cavity and you had a "hot plate" for heating another can or frying a disk of canned meat. It works. They break down quickly but C-rations come in cans.

He stood, frozen in place. To make the matter critical, in a few minutes the fire spread to the grass where his loaded M-16 lay with an elevated barrel. The fire could cause the rifle to fire or the ammunition in its magazine to explode and perhaps wound one of my men.

I sprinted to get the M-16 out of the fire before it fired. He tried to move it with weak kicking motions. This left it in the fire and turned it to point the barrel directly at me. Without slowing down, I reached the rifle and kicked it out of the fire. I stopped a few yards away. The fire did not have enough time to cause the rifle to fire or the ammunition in the magazine to "cook off."

I asked what was wrong. He told me he'd had received a "Dear John" letter from his wife. She wanted a divorce, which explained his hesitation and evident mental confusion. I had no choice but to replace him. When I receive or give orders in a combat situation, I need a quick-witted RTO. I couldn't take the chance he might freeze or become confused again.

Another Airstrike?

I received a radio call from my company commander about 10 o'clock in the morning. He gave me orders to move my platoon three kilometers away from Hill 15. Essentially, we'd be retracing the march that brought us to Hill 15. The reason for the move was the need to get us to a "safe distance," three thousand meters, from an airstrike scheduled for one of the hills on the opposite side of the river in an hour.

Having settled my orders, I asked my CO, with the greatest innocence, about the airstrike that took place at eight in the morning. After a moment's silence, followed by a question confirming what I had told him, he rescinded the new orders. Sort of like Gilda Radner's iconic "never mind" on the original *Saturday Night Live* television show. The military expression SNAFU comes to mind. For the uninitiated, SNAFU means Situation Normal All Fucked Up.

A Bomb Damage Assessment

Later, I received orders to board the helicopters coming to take us to the area the Air Force had bombed earlier in the morning. The Air Force wanted a bomb damage assessment of the morning's air strike on some fortifications.

We had the routine down pat. I ordered a smoke grenade thrown to the landing zone near Hill 15. The helicopters landed and we boarded them. The helicopters flew us over the river and landed at the base of the bombed hill. We spread out and started up to find where the bombs had struck. I knew in general the area where the F-100s delivered their bombs. We located the area bombed but climbing a hill thick with small trees, some brush and muddy slopes is not easy.

The F-100s not receiving any ground fire meant it was unlikely any Viet Cong were in the area. It also made meeting any enemy resistance while we climbed the hill unlikely. Only a fool would take such a chance. We went ready for whatever might happen.

The mission went well. We found the fortifications, a couple of bunkers. The closely packed trees made seeing them problematic from the air. The F-100s came close but completely missed them.

We found no bomb damage beyond craters in the muddy hillsides. The two small bunkers sustained no damage. We destroyed them and got completely muddy again. We gained a lot of experience destroying bunkers in mud.

The helicopters returned and airlifted us to a point closer to the company, completing an interesting, if not terribly productive day. That made it better than most days.

Forgotten Invitations to Bob Hope's Show

While we'd sat on Hill 15, I received some welcome news from the company commander; each platoon would have one man airlifted into Long Binh to watch Bob Hope's show. My men drew lots to see who would win. I did not draw because to me the show was for the men. We waited for the helicopter for a long time. No helicopter ever arrived to take a single paratrooper from D Company to see the Bob Hope Show.

The higher ups made a promise and broke it. The soldier who had won the drawing and every other man in the company had been forgotten. My company commander and I could do nothing about it.

From my perspective, what happened was, and remains, unforgivable. The news clips of Hope's shows from this period show clean-shaven men wearing clean jungle fatigues or other uniforms. Some of them called us "Boony Rats." We did too but with pride. We called them "REMFs" meaning "Rear Echelon Mother Fuckers." Every one of my "Boony Rats" earned a Combat Infantryman Badge for service in combat operations. The REMFs did not. It is a qualitative difference.

A Minor Contretemps with My Commander

Later, I received orders to bring my platoon to my company commander's command post. We marched there and arrived late in the afternoon. My CO told me he had orders to attend a conference at battalion headquarters. I was to take command of the company until he returned the next day. His last words to me before he got on the helicopter were, "Don't move the company!" He departed, leaving his rucksack behind. I didn't intend to move. No need existed to move from the dry mud free ridge.

After dark, I received a coded message from the battalion giving me a change in the boundaries of D Company's AO. It would be effective at 8 a.m. the next morning. I asked for and received a repeat of the coordinates and confirmation. I decoded it twice to make sure. They matched. I knew from the map coordinates I had to move the company, but I hoped drawing it on a map would prove me wrong. Not a chance!

Fortunately, the change was minimal, only shifting the boundaries two kilometers to the east. The positions of the other platoons in the unchanged part caused no difficulty but the move put the company's command post and my platoon's position outside of the new boundaries. I gave the other platoons the new boundaries.

After breakfast the next morning, I led my platoon and the men of the company command group to the closest point in the new AO. I carried my commander's rucksack in addition to my own. Mine was heavier but not by much. I had the other platoons meet us at the new location I'd designated for the company command post because it was our resupply day.

The helicopter arrived with our supplies and one pissed off company commander. His first words were "I told you not to move the company." I responded tersely that the battalion moved our AO two kilometers eastward last night, gave him the new coordinates and his rucksack, and asked leave to see to my platoon's resupply.

A Serious Problem with My Ordnance

During this resupply I noticed a heavy thumping against my left thigh. This alerted me to a problem. The safety handle on the white phosphorus grenade I carried had snapped off near the top. It now swung by the pull ring attached to its safety pin. The pin getting pulled did not concern me; I'd bent it to prevent it getting pulled accidently. I rechecked the pin just to be sure. What concerned me was how to get rid of the grenade.

The Army trains us to throw a fragmentation grenade thirty meters. But a white phosphorus grenade has a bursting radius of thirty-five meters, a five-meter shortfall for me. It also weighed twice as much as a fragmentation grenade. I didn't know if I could throw it far enough.

You hold the grenade's handle down by wrapping you fingers around it and the grenade. But the handle on this one was now a thumb-sized stub. The grenade training never covered dealing with a safety handle snapping off. I concluded trying to throw it farther carried too great a risk of a bad outcome. I found a deep, narrow gulley far from any of the company's men in which to detonate it, thus eliminating the bursting radius and throwing problems.

The deep gulley contained the explosion. I never carried another white phosphorus grenade. I was happy to leave the resupply point and my unhappy CO and get back to what I enjoyed most, leading the 1st Platoon.

Christmas Dinner 1968

Some days later, I received orders to rejoin the company near one of the paved roads running in and out of Long Binh. Trucks met us on one of them and drove us into Long Binh for Christmas dinner.

The mess hall was nice, as in pleasant looking and clean. Unfortunately, the mess hall staff did not appear glad to see us in their clean mess hall. I don't blame them. We wore jungle fatigues, which passed dirty days ago. We not only looked unwashed and unkempt, we smelled pretty bad from days of patrolling in the mud and rotting vegetation.

The mess hall's crew treated us professionally. They served us a delicious traditional Christmas dinner. We stuffed ourselves. If any one of them reads this, Thank You!

We returned to the rice paddies in our regular AO after a week of protecting Long Binh. The Bob Hope Show moved to its next venue. Once again, we patrolled the rice paddies and swamps west of Saigon. I needed a change from patrolling the same small piece of ground.

9

Extending My Tour
for Six More Months

20 March 1969

The End of My First Year in Vietnam

The end of my tour of duty in Vietnam was rapidly approaching. I had some decisions to make. Did I want to extend my tour in Vietnam for another six months? If so, did I want to stay with my brigade? If I extended, did I want to remain on airborne status by transferring to another airborne unit? Or did I want to go home? Ultimately, I decided to extend my tour with a transfer to the 173rd Airborne Brigade (SEP). SEP is short for separate. Technically the 3rd Brigade was also SEP.

The 173rd was stationed in the hills and mountains of the Central Highlands of the II Corps Area of South Vietnam at this time. They made history in the major battles around Dak To.

I sent in my first request to extend my tour of duty by six months in January 1969. The Army promptly lost it. My Date of Return from Over Seas (DROS) approached. I submitted a second request to extend my tour of duty in early February 1969. The Army promptly lost my second request too! My DROS was weeks away. Unable to take Fate's multiple blunt hints; I submitted a third request to extend my tour of duty.

The next day I received orders sending me back to the United States with a departure date in a month. My future assignment was to Special Troops at Sixth Army Headquarters at the Presidio of

San Francisco. I learned Special Troops has units like the Presidio's Military Band. I have no idea what the Army thought I, an Infantry paratrooper and combat veteran with the musical ability of tapioca pudding, could offer the band. Plus, I had not played a musical instrument in more than a decade.

Puzzled as I was, I was happy to receive the assignment. San Francisco was known as a party town. My company commander and I discussed this situation. Luckily, he wasn't pissed at me anymore. He said he would let me go as early as possible but he had limits on how early.

Orders rescinding my reassignment to the Presidio and my transfer to the 173rd arrived the next week, by TELETYPE. It occurred to me this was more a reprieve for the Sixth Army's band than Fate's way of saying "I warned you."

My orders included a provision for a Special Leave of thirty days. I decided to go home to Orange County, California, again. I was flown to Travis Air Force Base near San Francisco. I took a military bus to the San Francisco Airport and arranged to fly home. I took a taxi from John Wayne Airport in Orange County to my grandmother's home in the City of Orange. I'd get a ride home from there.

Nearly all of my family worked or went to school but I expected my grandmother to be home. Sometimes expectations aren't fulfilled. The front door was locked. The only option left to me was to walk to my family's home in Villa Park, a four-to-five-mile walk. I knew my family never locked the house. They lost their house keys repeatedly.

The walk didn't take long due to my excellent physical condition from slogging through the mud. When I arrived home, I saw the front door had not been locked. No one was home. I took an extra-long hot shower to wash off the dirt and smell of Vietnam, which had travelled with me on the long flight. Being clean and wearing clean clothes bring an indescribable feeling with them.

I watched television to pass the time. When my mother came home, she entered through the connecting door from the garage behind my chair. She immediately became irritated with me. I had forgotten we weren't supposed to sit in the naugahyde-covered chair without a shirt; it was something about the oils on skin ruining the material. She was angry because I was not wearing a shirt. She had not yet seen my face.

She stepped around and in front of me, literally stopped mid-word and did a double take. She'd confused me with my youngest brother David. He bears a resemblance to me. Realizing which of her sons sat in front of her, she gave me one of the strongest hugs I ever received from her. Unfortunately, it was around my neck and strong enough to choke me. In retrospect, I probably should have let someone know of my travel plans. I would have saved myself the expense of the taxi, a long walk and my mother choking me.

After she took a good look at me, she said, "You look terrible." I had never been in better shape in my life despite being down to about one hundred forty or fifty pounds. I also had a good tan from my outdoor life. Tact is not a hallmark of my family. This was my welcome home after my first year in Vietnam.

I brought with me as a souvenir a set of Vietnamese camouflage fatigues with all the appropriate insignias sewn on them. I acquired a set in a size large enough to fit me. They no longer fit me once I left Vietnam for good. I lost track of them years later. I had a photograph taken of me wearing them while standing in front of the house's front door. Except for the lack of mud on the uniform and on me, the photograph depicts me as a first lieutenant in the spring of 1969.

The thirty days went by quickly. I needed to return to Travis Air Force Base for a return flight to Vietnam. I did not return empty-handed. I brought a large bottle of Mateus wine and Genoa salami with me. Both retained the cold from the cargo hold of the return flight.

10

Farewell 3rd Brigade, Hello 173rd Brigade

20 March 1969

I arrived at Tan Son Nhut Air Base and hitched a ride to D Company's rear area on the far side of the airfield. I met with the company's first sergeant, our senior NCO (Non-Commissioned Officer) to begin processing out of D Company. But first, we shared the Mateus wine and the salami. The first sergeant produced some cheese and crackers to go with the wine and salami. We passed a fine hour talking about life, the war, and the military while we finished the wine and most of the sausage.

The company clerk had my transfer and travel orders ready for me when we finished the wine. I shook their hands and said my farewells. I never saw the first sergeant again. I do have a photograph of him taken on one of our resupply days. He was a fine NCO and gentleman of the old school.

I wanted to say goodbye to the 1st Platoon, D Company and General Bolling. This was not possible; the 3rd Brigade was engaged in an operation in War Zone D where many VC could still be found.

My transfer to the 173rd was a routine matter. Taking my M-16 with me was not. I decided I was not going to travel around Vietnam unarmed. The transfer of my rifle was literally a matter of bookkeeping. The 508th Battalion's Property Book Officer prepared the appropriate forms transferring the accountability for the weapon to the 173rd. I only needed to give them to the 173rd's Property Book

Officer and the transfer would be complete. This happened without a hitch. I learned how this worked in OCS.

I caught a ride on one of the U.S. Air Force's Canadian built C-7 Caribou cargo and troop transports to the 173rd Brigade's headquarters in Bong Son in II Corps. I traveled dressed for combat: steel helmet, load bearing harness with knife, water filled canteen and bladders, twenty-five loaded M-16 magazines in ammo pouches, two fragmentation grenades, two smoke grenades, a rucksack, a Lensatic compass, a map case, and a loaded M-16A1 assault rifle. This time I intended to arrive properly attired, armed and prepared for war.

PART Two

The 173rd Airborne Brigade

21 March 1969 to 9 March 1970

The Combat Service Identification Badge for the 173rd Airborne Brigade

11

LZ Uplift, Reconnaissance Missions, and a Life Saved

21 March 1969 to 12 June 1969

Getting to LZ Uplift

The flight on a C-7 Caribou from Tan Son Nhut Airbase turned out to be the flying equivalent of a cruise on a tramp steamer. The plane flew from tiny airfield to tiny airfield, dropped off passengers and cargo and took on more passengers. The flight was a learning experience for me. I saw an amazing amount of Vietnam, much more than the vast majority of the American ground forces ever saw. I enjoyed it immensely.

I arrived at the 173rd Airborne Brigade's Headquarters at Landing Zone (LZ) English, which was approximately three kilometers north of the town of Bong Son, Binh Dinh Province in II Corps.

I reported to the brigade's G-1 (Personnel). He assigned me to the 1st Battalion 503rd Parachute Infantry Regiment at LZ Uplift. According to the maps, it was located about nineteen kilometers south on National Route QL-1. The battalion S-1 further assigned me to lead E Company's Reconnaissance Platoon.

I knew I looked different from any other newly arriving first lieutenants. All of them wore new jungle fatigues. They also needed to be outfitted and equipped for war. I looked like I had just stepped out of the jungle. The 82nd Division's unit patch sewn onto my fatigue shirt's right shoulder said I had served in combat with it.

My loaded M-16A1 and grenades were obvious clues. Some clues were subtler. My rucksack showed two quick releases instead of the standard one; pull both and it instantly dropped away. My clear plastic map case hidden in my left thigh pocket was not obvious either. I only lacked a platoon to lead and the necessary maps to allow me to lead them to our objectives. I stood ready for combat.

The 1st Battalion's AO covered a coastal plain bound by the South China Sea on the east and low hills rising to the mountains of the Central Highlands in the west. On the coastal plain, primarily an agricultural area, local farmers grew rice as their principal crop. The villages along the coastline caught fish as their principal product. The people clustered in small villages of thatched huts.

Several interconnecting valleys, which bore few signs of habitation or farming, divided the hills surrounding the coastal plain. Our maps showed villages scattered through them. All evidence of those villages had vanished without a trace a long time ago. One remaining village lay about one hundred yards from the perimeter wire of LZ Uplift.

Commanding a Reconnaissance Platoon

I was given command of E Company's Reconnaissance Platoon. A reconnaissance platoon is structured and equipped differently than a rifle platoon. Instead of three rifle squads and a weapons squad with two M-60 machine gun teams, it consisted of four reconnaissance teams. Each team consisted of six men instead of the ten in a rifle squad. A typical team had one team leader, a sergeant, an assistant team leader and four riflemen, all armed with M-16 rifles. One M-60 machine gun was optional in lieu of an M-16.

Teams used the same radio as the rifle platoons, a PRC-25. The radio's nominal transmission and reception range of twelve to fifteen kilometers kept the teams and the battalion in radio contact, depending on the terrain, elevation and weather. The PRC-25 provided a large frequency selection. You tuned to one by turning a dial much like a car radio.

By this time the brigade had received electronic encryption devices, which allowed a PRC-25 to transmit and receive encrypted radio traffic between the brigade, the battalions and the companies. They worked like scramblers. The code settings for the devices changed daily. Neither the rifle platoons nor the recon teams received these devices.

The RTO usually carried his PRC-25 rigged in his rucksack. He clipped his telephone-style handset high on his load-bearing harness next to his ear. He could keep the volume low and not have it give us away to an enemy. But he could hear all the radio traffic on our frequency. It provided good clear reception or transmission in most instances. It was literally the lifeline for any unit in the field.

The battalion deployed the recon teams to act as its eyes and ears in the areas beyond those reconnoitered by the rifle companies. Their basic mission was to locate the enemy troop concentrations or signs of enemy activity or enemy movement, and report back to the battalion. Their secondary job was to locate trails, fortifications, weapon and ammunition caches, or anything unusual.

The teams generally operated under instructions to avoid becoming engaged in combat. Getting into a firefight gave away their presence to the enemy, which ended the mission. They often patrolled too far from the rifle companies for rapid reinforcement. Plus, a six-man team is too weak to stand up to more than a handful of the enemy. Instead of scouting, they might find themselves running for their lives.

The teams ordinarily operated independently. But rare occasions arose when two or more teams would be sent into the same area, primarily for reasons of self-defense in a more distant than usual location, or possibly because the area contained a substantial number of the enemy. It is simple math: twelve men had a far better chance of defending themselves than six did.

The platoon leader of a reconnaissance platoon does not spend a lot of time in the field. I never expected this and never fully adjusted. My role was to prepare the teams for their upcoming missions. This included defining the mission, the time frame, their objectives, and the details of extraction. The battalion's intelligence officer briefed them on the enemy forces in the area of their mission and conducted a map reconnaissance of the area where they were headed.

I did not enjoy all the time out of the field. I really enjoyed leading an Infantry platoon because we could scout a large area fairly quickly and engage small enemy units.

We went to some trouble to disguise the insertions of the teams because a helicopter is a loud aircraft. When possible, we airlifted a team to an existing manned position where they could simply walk a short distance out to the jungle or forest and disappear.

We also used helicopters with closed doors to make multiple landings in the area. Upon landing in or near their recon area, the team opened the doors and jumped out. The helicopter took off when the doors closed. We hoped to fool the enemy as to the actual point of the insertion. It worked more often than you might expect.

I went with teams on missions using some of those insertion techniques. It felt different to have only six men with me rather than the thirty to thirty-five in my understrength rifle platoons. I disliked the restricted options in the event we encountered an enemy force. The teams found fortifications, trails, water sources; on one occasion triggered a Viet Cong booby trap, and on another occasion encountered two Viet Cong.

One of my team leaders, a sergeant who had served two prior tours of duty in Vietnam, showed me some new tricks for our ambushes. The best one turned the tables on an enemy soldier sneaking up in the dark to turn our directional Claymore mines to point at us. They hoped we would wound or kill ourselves when we set them off. This happened to some rifle platoons and rifle companies.

The sergeant attached a trip wire from a ground flare to each Claymore. Turning the mine pulls the flare's pin. The brief click, followed by the instant burst of a blinding light, told the sergeant to detonate the Claymore. An enemy infiltrator wouldn't survive, especially if he held the Claymore in his hands.

During a mission with this sergeant, we came across the main rotor blade and the rocket pod of a helicopter gunship. They lay in a small bowl-like crease between some low hilltops. The bowl was surrounded by a moderately dense forest of small trees and saplings. The rocket pod contained a full complement of rockets with warheads. We searched for a second rocket pod without success. We dutifully reported the find to battalion saying we would return to destroy the rockets when we completed our mission.

Battalion ordered us to destroy it at once. We tried again to get permission to complete our mission first but battalion again said no, adding they were readying the explosives and related items to bring to us to destroy the rocket pod. The explosives came by helicopter, which immediately gave away our position. We required extraction once we destroyed the warheads.

We rigged the rocket pod with all the explosives we received, far more than necessary. We detonated the explosives and the rockets without any injuries. I went back to see the condition of the rocket pod. It had disappeared. I never located any fragments.

The explosion blew the leaves off of every tree and sapling inside or immediately surrounding the bowl. Those tree leaves and fragments of leaves completely carpeted the bowl with a soft green layer of shredded leaves. Afterward, we went to the extraction point.

We used a different method of insertion when I went with one of the other teams to reconnoiter the western hills of the valley connecting LZ Uplift to an artillery base northwest of us. We had reason to believe the NVA were crossing the valley to reach the coastal areas to the east. The helicopter landed us a few hundred meters from the artillery base and close to the end of a ridge from the western hills where the valley from LZ Uplift joined another valley. The other valley opened to the west.

We began the climb of the ridge's slope immediately. It was slow and hard going up a steep slope covered by a moderately thick forest. It took us about an hour of climbing to reach the top of the ridge, which ran along the top of the hills. Thanks to the foliage, the heat and the humidity, we were soaked with sweat from climbing up the slope.

We followed the ridge to the south. We soon found some recent bomb damage. A large bomb, or maybe two, blew away a dozen or more large trees and a large part of the hillside on the west side of the ridge. I thought it odd that anyone thought it worthwhile to cause damage of that magnitude when we saw no signs of enemy activity nearby.

I stood at the top edge of the crater to scan the hills to the west. Those closely set hills, covered by the thick forest, offered the NVA any number of concealed routes into our AO. I made a mental note to raise the idea of sending teams to reconnoiter them.

We continued along the ridgeline until we saw the outlines of dozens of concealed fortifications through the tree leaves and the undergrowth. The mission brief included nothing about them. This implied they had likely remained undiscovered by American or South Vietnamese forces. We approached cautiously, trying to remain concealed, until we could see if they held enemy troops. They were unoccupied.

We proceeded further into the fortifications but very carefully lest we trip booby traps. We found no enemy forces or booby traps throughout the entire area. From their general appearance of neglect, no large enemy forces had occupied them for a long time, further evidence of the NVA's huge losses in their Tet Offensive of 1968. Physically, the fortifications were still serviceable. We spread out to determine their size and number.

The dozens of fortifications consisted of bunkers partially buried in the ground. The construction was the usual log walls with log and packed earth roofs to provide protection from bombs and artillery shells. I'd seen similar bunkers south of Saigon and outside of Long Binh. The thick roofs could withstand the explosion of a hand grenade or a rocket but weren't thick enough to protect the enemy from direct hits or near misses by artillery shells or bombs. Their depth provided protection from rifle and machine gun fire or not so near misses by artillery shells, rockets or bombs.

Each roof was slightly elevated above ground level. This provided the defenders with excellent views for firing downhill or to their flanks. The size of the bunkers ranged from big enough for two men to big enough for four to six men. The entrance to each bunker was uniformly in the rear, their uphill side. These bunkers were clearly intended to defend against an attack up the steep slope to their front and secondarily from attacks along the ridgeline on their flanks.

An uphill attack directly at the bunkers would be suicide for the attackers. An attack along the ridgeline on their flanks offered a serious possibility of success, especially if the uphill wing of the attack reached the extreme rear of the fortifications. In such a case the fortifications would become death traps for the defenders. An attack up the steep rear slope could easily succeed but only if undetected before it gained the ridge. The loss of surprise could turn the assault into a major battle.

I saw no signs of recent use by individuals or small groups. It also showed no signs of rocket, artillery or bomb damage. This implied the possibility the NVA believed the presence of the fortifications remained their secret, to be used whenever they regained their strength. To destroy them required engineers; we had neither the numbers nor tools nor the explosives for the job. Later, I suggested an air strike or concentrated artillery fire to destroy it. Nothing was done, if I remember correctly.

We found a small trickle of water ten meters downhill from the lowest bunkers. It bubbled up from a small rock formation. The flow created a tiny but steady stream of water downhill but got a little bigger further down the hill where another trickle joined the flow. The water, clear and cool, provided enough water for the number of men who could man those bunkers, if they showed some water discipline.

Their problem was its location outside of the fortified area. This made it extremely risky to reach in a firefight, which caused me to believe the primary function for the bunkers was to provide daytime shelter and protection for a transiting enemy force of several hundred. At night, they could rapidly proceed downhill, cross the narrow valley floor, and climb the hills on the east side of the valley. The populated coastal area would lie open to them once they reached the bottom of the east side of those hills.

Alternatively, the jungle-covered ridgeline on the east side of the valley offered an attack force a concealed way to approach to within two hundred meters of LZ Uplift's defensive perimeter. We'd get little warning before the attack began.

We followed the flow of water downhill to discover anything else of interest along the flow. We found nothing more. I made a note of it for later, drawing it on the maps in the battalion's Tactical Operations Center (TOC). The fortifications were the high point of the mission. We'd found where the NVA crossed the valley on the way to the coastal plain.

A Team Trips a Booby Trap and Two Are Wounded; and a Hot Dog

The battalion's operations officer wanted us to reconnoiter a particular area to look for signs of enemy activity. I sent the next team in the rotation on that mission. Two days into the mission one of the men tripped a booby trap. It exploded, wounding him and the team leader walking behind him. They were picked up by a "Dust-off," aka medevac UH-1 helicopter rigged for medical evacuation of wounded soldiers. Another UH-1 helicopter extracted the remainder of the team.

The medevac flew the team leader to the Army Evacuation Hospital in Qui Nhon because his injuries, while serious, did not threaten his life or a major organ. A piece of shrapnel passed through one of his cheeks and out the other, knocking out a couple teeth during its passage through his mouth. The medevac continued on with the second man directly to a hospital ship sailing off the coast. His more serious injury had a life altering aspect to it.

The company commander, another first lieutenant, who commanded the reconnaissance platoon before me, and I drove to the Army Evacuation Hospital in Qui Nhon to visit the wounded team leader with two unspoken goals. We wanted to see how he was doing and if he needed anything. We also brought messages from his comrades to deliver and planned to carry any messages he wanted us to take back to them.

We try to check up on our wounded for these reasons to demonstrate their well-being is important to us and because they are colleagues and often friends. We want them to know we have not forgotten them.

He looked to be in good condition. The surgeons sutured the entry and exit wounds in his cheeks. The oral surgeons had cleaned up and repaired the damage to his jaw and gums caused by the shrapnel fragment, which knocked out a tooth or two. Soon they'd transfer him to an Army hospital with dentists skilled in reconstruction of the damage to his mouth. He spoke well if carefully to avoid tearing any stitches. The three of us enjoyed a good visit.

He told us he was hungry. He could not have solid food because of the damage to his mouth. The doctors had him on intravenous feeding. Consequently, his stomach sent many messages to his brain telling him to eat something. The company commander and I saw only a wounded paratrooper sorely in need of food.

With my commander's agreement, I slipped out to the hot dog stand outside the hospital's entrance. I bought a hot dog with the condiments our paratrooper wanted on it. I smuggled it into his ward. He had eaten about half of the hot dog when one of the nurses, a short blonde second lieutenant caught us. I'd heard the other nurses calling her "Thumper." I never learned the reason behind her nickname.

Thumper told us off and shook her finger at two first lieutenants who towered over her and outranked her. We told her we were sorry (we weren't) and would never do it again (we would). Satisfied with the strong message she delivered, she left with the remnants of the hot dog. We finished our visit and returned to LZ Uplift. Not long after the hot dog incident, doctors sent my paratrooper back to the United States for additional treatment by dental specialists.

The other paratrooper was evacuated from the hospital ship to a military hospital in Japan because of the serious nature of his injury coupled with the greater ability of the surgeons there to repair it. His injury, while not life threatening, had a tremendous potential to be life altering. A piece of shrapnel had struck his penis and caused some unspecified damage. This is an important issue for men.

He had nicknamed his penis "Theodore." I don't know why. The platoon received a letter from him about two weeks after his injury. He wrote about his extreme concern that Theodore did not move. His simple words could not have begun to describe the true level of his worry, a concern apparently shared by his doctors. Surgery became necessary to repair the damage. The platoon received a one-line postcard from him a month later; it simply read, "Theodore moved." He was going to be okay! Sometime later they sent him home to finish recovering.

Reconnaissance of the Village Outside of Our Perimeter

I usually remained at LZ Uplift, which is boring for someone accustomed to being in the field. The village, only a hundred yards outside our perimeter defenses, made me nervous. It offered the enemy another possible close approach to our defenses without exposing themselves to detection. I decided to infiltrate it one night and listen for any activity threatening LZ Uplift. After midnight, I led two of my men and the battalion's communications or signals officer, another first lieutenant and a friend, out through the gate on the south side of LZ Uplift.

We took a circuitous route through the high brush around the village to avoid detection until we reached the point where the thick brush grew down to the edge of the rice paddies. We crawled along the wet muddy paddy dykes for the last hundred meters to the village. This reminded me of the many similar muddy situations I experienced around Saigon.

One of my men whispered more than once "You guys are crazy." The other lieutenant and I responded "Shush" as we crawled along the paddy dyke. He spoke his last "You guys are crazy" when we reached the edge of the village. I held a finger to my lips to signal silence and pointed to the thatched hut fifteen feet away. I could hear someone snoring inside.

We lay still and listened for any signs or sounds of movement around the village. The village dogs helped us by barking at strangers in the village, which they did when we tried to creep a little bit closer. They stopped barking when we stopped moving.

We stayed for nearly an hour, heard no sounds of movement except for the snoring and occasional dog barking. We left the way we came. I felt a little better knowing the village dogs barked at strangers.

My friend, the signals officer, who wanted to be an Infantry officer, got his wish to command a rifle platoon in combat operations. Sadly, I heard he was killed in action. The world and Boston lost a good man and extremely funny Irishman.

A Meeting with a Viet Cong VIP and His Bodyguard

The next reconnaissance mission held a little more excitement for the team I accompanied. A helicopter landed us at a different firebase in the morning. We usually deployed during twilight. That day we walked out of the firebase and disappeared into the jungle. We made our way downhill through the jungle. Thirty minutes later we reached a small creek. We hadn't seen any trails or signs of enemy movement through the thick jungle. The creek bed looked like a wide stony hallway with jungle walls.

Since we hadn't come across any trails, I decided to follow the creek for the few hundred meters to where the creek met the valley floor, a large open area where two valleys met.

I ordered the team leader to take two men to reconnoiter where it met the valley floor because the three men could remain out of sight easier than seven. We had to cross this open area. I did not want to be surprised since our options were not particularly good.

Less than five minutes had passed when I heard M-16s firing fully automatic. The sound came from downstream where my men had gone. I did not hear the sounds of an AK-47 being fired. I knew the difference.

I told the RTO to let battalion know we had engaged the enemy. I told him and the rest of the team to follow me downstream once battalion had acknowledged the message. I immediately dropped my rucksack and took off downstream as fast as possible.

It was a classic meeting engagement. My three men had met two Viet Cong heading upstream. The meeting resulted in a brief burst of gunfire. My men were quicker. One unarmed Viet Cong died. The one armed with an AK-47 fled without firing a shot. I searched for him along his direction of flight without success. I returned to where the dead Viet Cong lay.

He had been hit in the head, which blew off part of his skull. His brain and the inside of his brain case were exposed. He had a satchel containing documents in Vietnamese, which we seized for the battalion's intelligence officer. We went through his pockets, seized everything he carried for whatever intelligence value it contained.

It turned out the dead VC was the assistant finance chief for the VC's shadow Province Government in our area. A Province is somewhat like a county. Those documents were his financial records. This chance encounter provided us with a great deal of intelligence on the shadow government. Our intelligence officer told me the records described the dead man's discovery of the embezzlement of the equivalent of about thirty thousand dollars in Viet Cong Province funds. I believe those records contained names but I didn't need to know them.

An Ersatz Criminal Defense Lawyer

I said I didn't see a lot of fieldwork. This gave battalion the opportunity to give me special assignments. One of those made me defense counsel for a soldier accused of striking a commissioned officer. He faced a Special Court Martial. At this time, an accused soldier did not get a lawyer to assist with his defense at special court martial. The prosecution also did not have a lawyer. They got any available officer instead, usually a lieutenant. With me, he didn't even get a college graduate.

A special court martial can impose fines, demotion, a six-month period of incarceration and a bad conduct discharge. Modernly, the available punishments are limited and real lawyers serve as defense counsel and prosecutor.

My "client" worked hard to make my job impossible. The year 1969 saw a great deal of racial friction between African American and Caucasian soldiers because not all of the remnants of the legacies of slavery and segregation had been eliminated in the United States. These legacies were being slowly eliminated in America. The military was doing it faster than the nation but they were not finished

My client was African American while I was Caucasian. He carried an abiding hatred and distrust of all Caucasians, including me. Try as I might, and I did many times, I could not gain his trust and cooperation in telling me his version of what transpired. I desperately needed his help to locate witnesses who could testify on his behalf or allow me to rebut the officer's version of the events. I saw a good chance to beat the charge or at least avoid the stigma of a bad conduct discharge.

My view of this case is now colored by my years as a practicing lawyer. The case swam in reasonable doubt. I did not have the knowledge and skill to prove that fact. I wonder how many other cases like this reached questionable outcomes.

The incident occurred at the end of a barracks fight with multiple participants and witnesses. I talked with the officer, a Caucasian and an acquaintance. I obtained his complete story of the event. He'd heard the fight in the enlisted men's quarters and entered to break it up. He got struck in the process of separating the combatants.

An unwritten rule said officers should leave these things to the sergeants. Had he called for a sergeant, this charge and a special court martial would not have been necessary.

This is where reasonable doubt comes in. The prosecutor needed to prove this soldier knew he was hitting a commissioned officer. The description of the fight sounded like a melee, a confused fight. In the confusion, it's quite possible he swung at another combatant, missed and hit the officer by mistake.

I could make credible arguments my client acted under the adrenaline rush of a fist fight and did not realize an officer stood nearby before striking him or thought it was another soldier attacking him. I needed my client to talk with me about what happened. I needed him to give me his witnesses. He refused time after time.

I interviewed the rest of the combatants in the barracks but with all the fighting no one saw the part that concerned me or would admit to seeing it. Without my client's assistance, I couldn't get through to the men who might help him.

The court martial went as expected. The officer testified against my client. I had no witnesses, which left me with nothing but posing pathetic questions to the officer and an oral argument. The Court Martial Board found him guilty. He received the maximum punishment, including the bad conduct discharge. The black mark of a bad conduct discharge would stay with him throughout his life.

An Ersatz Criminal Prosecuting Attorney

My next Special Court Martial found me assigned as the prosecutor. The charge was being Absent Without Leave (AWOL). The accusation stated the man did not go to the hospital in Qui Nhon for treatment, as ordered. This is not a serious enough charge to warrant a Special Court Martial. Qui Nhon is about thirty kilometers southeast of LZ Uplift on National Route QL-1.

I saw immediately I needed to prove he wasn't treated at the hospital. One way to do this was the hospital records. Time for another road trip. Fortunately for me, National Route QL-1 is a well-traveled road between LZ Uplift and Qui Nhon. All I had to do was hitch a ride on a passing Army truck. I had done this more than once.

In his statement to his CO, the paratrooper said he'd gone to the hospital and got his treatment. I personally spoke to the military police who controlled access to the hospital. From them I learned they kept no records of soldiers arriving or leaving the hospital. They could not offer anything to prove he had or had not come to the hospital on the day in question. The hospital had the same problem with its records. I understood this was not an uncommon situation involving a sensitive ailment, an STD, like this soldier had.

I saw I wasn't going to overcome the presumption of innocence. He might have gone to the hospital but I had to prove beyond a reasonable doubt he had not. I hitchhiked back to LZ Uplift.

I reported the results of my investigation to the battalion commander, the convening authority for the special court martial. I suggested, respectfully, that he withdraw the charge. I got the disturbing impression that he really wanted to hang that paratrooper out to dry. I couldn't put that question to him. I never learned the reason he wanted this man punished.

A case of AWOL is usually handled at the company level with an Article 15 (Non-Judicial Punishment) before the company commander. It's part of the Uniform Code of Military Justice. It's an administrative procedure and leaves no permanent mark on the soldier's record. The punishments are much lower and there is no possibility of receiving a sentence to jail or a bad conduct discharge.

I explained the existence of strong reasonable doubt of the soldier's guilt to the battalion commander. He took this poorly. I overcame his reluctance to my suggestion to drop the AWOL charge; he grudgingly dropped the charge. To me, the charges and pending special court martial had been a colossal waste of time. I want to win, but fairly.

The special court martial itself was overkill and a gross miscarriage of justice for a first-time charge of AWOL. Such a miscarriage of justice hurts troop morale. I did not think of the situation in those exact terms then but this is the substance of my thoughts. Now, decades later, as a real lawyer, I do think of it in those terms and more.

The final score in my first foray into criminal litigation was zero wins, two losses, hardly an auspicious beginning. I did succeed in preventing a colossal injustice. Perhaps I should count this as a win.

Sitting on a Court-Martial

I was called to sit on a special court-martial board in the capacity of one of three officers acting as judges and jury. The trials we heard involved minor offenses warranting a reduction in rank or fines or both but no discharge of any type and no time in jail. The prosecution won, as it usually did. The unfairness of these situations finally persuaded the Congress, or forced it, to make the changes I mentioned earlier. It is fairer but the prosecution still wins the majority of its cases as happens in the civilian criminal courts.

The Rescue Flight

I rode in a lot of helicopters, another form of hitchhiking, on a variety of administrative assignments. One of those flights was different. I shared a UH-1 with a lieutenant colonel and a major. I do not recall where they were going but it would drop me off at LZ Uplift. Rank hath its privileges; the field grade officers sat on the bench seat. I sat on the floor.

The door gunner let me know we were diverting to evacuate a sick paratrooper from one of the brigade's rifle companies and fly him to brigade hospital at LZ English. This was an emergency situation with no medevac helicopter available for an immediate pickup. We were only minutes away. I believe the pilot volunteered to make the pickup.

We landed. A small group of soldiers carried one of their comrades to the helicopter. The medic got my attention. To overcome the engine and main rotor noise, he yelled into my ear. He said the unconscious man was a poor soldier but he suffered from heat stroke and had stopped breathing several times and required mouth-to-mouth resuscitation each time. The medic wanted me to watch the soldier in case he stopped breathing again. The helicopter took off once the man was safely inside with me to keep watch over him. We were not on the ground more than a minute.

I was surprised the medic made no attempt to inform the lieutenant colonel or the major. I put it down to the fact that I, an Infantry lieutenant, was the only one of the three commissioned officers from whom he could expect help.

The flight to LZ English took a handful of minutes but I was too focused to keep track of the time. I kept a close eye on the paratrooper. It was hard to tell if he was breathing or not; the helicopter generated too much vibration, noise and wind to make an accurate determination. I thought he stopped two times. At least his chest looked like it stopped moving. I gave him mouth-to-mouth to resuscitate him. I did it correctly. It worked, I think, at least his chest began to move again. All other times, I poured water from my canteen over his head and chest to try to keep him as cool as possible.

Medics at LZ English met us when we landed and I passed on the information the field medic had given me. I never knew the soldier's name or how he fared. The two higher-ranking officers did nothing to help me. Their faces held disapproving looks when I gave the man mouth-to-mouth resuscitation. Maybe they thought the man was a malingerer and deserved heat stroke. Maybe they disapproved because the man happened to be African American.

Neither made any difference. He was a soldier like them and me. We are expected to take care of each other. The senior officers' attitude was somehow disconcerting as it contradicted the principle behind the bond between soldiers. I do not pretend to be flawless. Just ask my wife. But there are times when it is necessary to put such bullshit aside.

The First Command Failure Lets Viet Cong Get 400-Plus Claymore Mines

How did the Viet Cong get their hands on more than four hundred Claymores mines? The answer is interservice stupidity. I'd been in the TOC when the first notification of the incident arrived and heard the Army side of the ridiculous bickering begin.

This happened during a stormy night. We received word a U.S. Navy Landing Craft carrying more than four hundred U.S. Claymore anti-personnel mines had been beached on the coast in our AO. It was about five kilometers (3.1 miles) from LZ Uplift. The Navy asked us to secure it. We had excellent options. We had a rifle company in the area. A rifle platoon could have reached the landing craft very quickly. Trucks or armored vehicles at LZ Uplift could cross the distance in a few minutes. My men and I could be combat ready and in the trucks in less than ten minutes.

The 1st Battalion's incompetent CO repeatedly refused to take action. He stood firm on, "It's the Navy's problem." While he and the Navy bickered over who bore the responsibility for securing the landing craft, the VC helped themselves to our Claymore mines.

The result was American soldiers being injured and killed by the Claymore mines the VC used against us. American soldiers were periodically wounded and killed by them for months. I don't know how many.

Many months later, I saw the beached and rusting landing craft. As far as I know, it's still rusting away in the surf line in case anyone wants to see it. It should be declared a U.S. monument to interservice stupidity.

A Second Command Failure Leaves My Recon Team Twisting in the Wind

This command failure took place when I'd led the recon platoon for about three months. Around midnight, the team leader of a deployed team reported sounds around them like an enemy force was moving closer to them. Fortunately, his team remained undetected. He made the decision to move his team away from their position.

The difficulty he faced was if he could hear them moving, they could hear his men if they moved and open fire on them. To cover the sound of his team's movement, he requested some artillery be fired at a point about four hundred meters away. Ordinarily, this is a simple request. This situation had nothing ordinary about it.

The battalion commander, the same one with the problem with the AWOL soldier and who refused to secure those four hundred Claymore mines in the beached U.S. Navy landing craft, was not at the battalion's Forward Command Post. He had returned to LZ Uplift where I was. The Battalion Executive Officer (XO), a major and sort of a bumbler, was at the Forward Command Post in his stead. The battalion commander left it to the XO to handle the problem and went back to bed. Unfortunately, the XO was incapable of making a decision.

The Artillery Liaison Officer, a captain, was having difficulty in obtaining clearance to fire the mission. The team was in a No Fire Zone. This meant he had to obtain political clearance from the South Vietnamese to fire the artillery support mission. This takes time, which passed quickly with no clearance from the Vietnamese.

My team leader continued to request the artillery fire, unaware of the command failure or the political situation. He reported the noises getting closer to their position. I gathered he became more insistent with each new request for artillery fire support. I knew him; he was a steady man not given to overstatement or panic. I trusted him completely.

I was in the main TOC in the rear listening to these radio transmissions. I could hear only one side of the broadcast because the radios in the Forward Command Post were powerful enough. The team's radio was out of range. I could not comprehend how a small unit in the field, requesting help, could be left twisting in the wind. This bore no resemblance to the U.S. Army I saw in action outside Hué. I said as much in no uncertain terms. Looking back, I am pretty sure I was caustic because I still recount it caustically today.

I probably said some things beyond caustic. I'm part Irish and have the temper to prove it. The lack of concern for my men and the incompetence really set me off. I could do nothing to help my men. This pushed me to the point of madness.

The artillery captain, like me, had grown increasingly frustrated with the situation. Ultimately, he bypassed the political clearance, contacted the artillery battery directly and told it to fire the mission. They fired; my team moved to safety under cover of the noise. They left their rucksacks behind to move quicker.

The next day a rifle platoon was sent to reconnoiter the area for signs of an enemy presence. It failed to find any sign of an enemy presence around the team's position. They did find my team's rucksacks where the team left them. The platoon ransacked them for anything that appeared worth taking.

I heard the artillery captain was relieved of his assignment. He sacrificed his career to help my team when nobody else would. For his act, and the moral courage it represented, I will be eternally grateful to him.

The battalion commander sent for me the next day. It seems my accurate but ill-considered remarks had been reported to him and rightly so. He proposed to transfer me to a rifle platoon for more seasoning. This statement spoke volumes about him. Obviously, he'd not read my personnel file. I doubt he'd taken the time to read the personnel files of any of his subordinate officers.

If he'd read mine, he'd have known I was not a green replacement but a combat veteran fresh from a year in Vietnam when I came to the battalion. I'd already earned the Combat Infantryman Badge sewn onto my fatigue shirt.

I told him "No Sir, just transfer me out of this battalion." I'm certain the tone of my voice conveyed my assessment of his capabilities as a field commander, or lack thereof. I do not recall trying to hide it.

This battalion commander had no prior Vietnam service. This pointed to him being a staff lifer. We called them lifers, a term of disrespect. I didn't consider him as anything but incompetent as a battalion commander. It is not a lieutenant's position to be critical of his superiors, but I served under a brilliant brigade commander in the 3rd Brigade of the 82nd Airborne Division. This battalion commander did not measure up to that standard, not even close.

This lieutenant colonel also had little comprehension of basic procedures, like regularly changing radio frequencies, call signs and codes. I attended the daily briefings the staff gave him. The battalion signal officer, the same one who had snuck up to that village with me, was responsible for keeping the communications system in good working order and the radio frequencies, call signs and codes up to date. The brigade allocated specified radio frequencies, call signs and codes to every unit, down to company level. Each had its own radio frequency and call signs. These changed every month for operation security and communication security reasons, i.e., to keep an enemy from knowing anything about our activities and operations.

At the beginning of every month, my friend briefed the battalion commander and staff on new changes to radio frequencies, codes and specifically his new call sign. This particular lieutenant couldn't understand why the number in his call sign had been changed. My friend, employing increasingly simple language, tried to explain to him the security concerns behind the monthly changes. He tried three times.

My friend finally gave up and told the battalion commander if he wanted his old call sign, he could have it. The less than respectful tone of his voice and the physical mannerism he displayed as he said those words spoke volumes. The battalion commander failed to recognize the disrespect.

The leadership classes in OCS stressed a good officer tries to know something about his subordinates, particularly his subordinate leaders. I concluded his incompetence posed a danger to all of us and I could not change that fact. I needed to be elsewhere. This was why I used a tone that manifestly expressed how little I thought of him or his command abilities. This is called insubordination. I could have faced a court-martial for the disrespectful tone of my voice.

Within a day or two, I sat in a helicopter taking me to the 3rd Battalion of the 503rd PIR. I already knew my new assignment, to command another understrength airborne rifle platoon in "C" Company. Finally, I would see what combat operations in the Central Highlands were like. Once again, it felt like I was going home.

This is a good point to discuss a disturbing phenomenon taking place within the ranks of the Army in 1969. The early signs the war was winding down had become more apparent. The Army began to identify various units, including Infantry battalions, to be sent home and not replaced. The 3rd Brigade, 82nd Airborne Division returned to Ft. Bragg after twenty-two months in Vietnam; three months before my last extension was completed.

A number of Infantry lieutenant colonels, "hiding out," in my estimation, in staff jobs around the world, suddenly realized the coming threat to their careers. If they were to have any chance of being promoted to full colonel, they needed their records to reflect they'd commanded an Infantry battalion in Vietnam. They worked the system to get one of those coveted assignments. I'd already seen two of them.

12

"C" Company, 3rd Battalion, 503rd PIR

June 12, 1969, to November 19, 1969

The 3rd Battalion operated separate from the brigade at this time. It was based on Pleiku Air Base, which lay about one hundred twenty kilometers (seventy-five miles) southwest of the brigade's headquarters at Bong Son. Pleiku is deep in the Central Highlands. The 3rd Battalion's mission was to patrol the area around the Air Base, detect any enemy threat to the base, and destroy the threat if possible. This mirrored similar missions I performed outside Saigon and Long Binh with the 3rd Brigade of the 82nd Airborne Division.

The differences? The 3rd Battalion was closer to the Ho Chi Minh Trail than to brigade headquarters. We operated in a drier and cooler climate, in hills, and mountainous country where dense jungles and forests were the rule and not the exception. The jungles grew at the lower elevations; the forests grew at the higher elevations.

"C" Company's CO, a captain, greeted me warmly. He had me work with a platoon commanded by a sergeant first class, aka platoon sergeant, for a few days. It helped me become acclimated to the enemy threat in the area, to the highlands and patrolling in the hills, mountains and valleys.

I have good memories of those few days and this platoon sergeant. What stands out about him, besides his competence, took place on an otherwise quiet afternoon. We saw a flight of four Air

140

Force F-100 fighter-bombers streak low overhead and deeper into the mountains beyond which lay the Ho Chi Minh Trail. They flew low enough that we could see that each of them carried a good-sized bomb, perhaps five hundred pounders, at every hard point on each wing for a total of eight per aircraft.

The platoon sergeant uttered one of the most memorable wartime understatements I've ever heard, "Its looks like they are going out to gang fuck somebody." Crude and insensitive, most assuredly, nonetheless it is an accurate and concise summation of something about to take place somewhere not far from us that day perhaps within 40 kilometers (25 miles). Shortly thereafter, the company commander handed command of the 1st Platoon to me. I was home.

Peace, Serenity and Dead Viet Cong

The highlands were a relief from the high heat and humidity of the lowlands and swamps I experienced around Saigon. Any land deserving the term flat could only be found in the valley floors between the hills and mountains. It was the same story; our maps depicted occasional villages in those valleys but again no signs of them existed anymore.

One of the most beautiful areas of the world I have ever seen was a tea plantation in the Central Highlands. The low hills made a sort of large bowl for the plantation. The mountains further west made an impressive backdrop for the hills. The floor of the bowl was a low hill itself. It and the hillsides surrounding it were terraced with thousands of tea plants. It looked much like a vineyard.

The tea plants were a truly beautiful green. I cannot describe it accurately, but I saw a kind of medium green, restful and easy on the eyes. The picture was made all the more memorable by a clear blue sky dotted with scattered white clouds. The temperature was comfortable with a light breeze of clean, fresh air. I could have been standing in a picture postcard scene.

This scene stood out spectacularly against the backdrop of the

Vietnam War. It conveyed a sense of serenity and peace. I had not experienced this in my travels through nearly two thirds of the country. We left the scene to continue my platoon's never-ending marches to engage the enemy. This is the military's way of saying we wanted to get into a firefight. The memory of that scene remains fresh. To the best of my knowledge the men with me that day made it out alive and in one piece.

The overall impression of peace and tranquility was marred by the dead bodies of four or five VC stacked beside one of the small, narrow packed dirt roads running through the plantation. One of the 3rd Battalion's reconnaissance teams killed them in a firefight.

The distance between the reconnaissance team and the enemy during the firefight was less than twenty-eight feet. I can say this with absolute confidence because one 40mm grenade fired by their grenadier had caved in the side of one man's skull without exploding. A 40mm grenade is designed to spin-arm itself once it leaves the grenade launcher. It must travel twenty-eight feet after being fired before it can detonate. I learned this in Infantry OCS. It hadn't traveled the twenty-eight feet necessary to arm itself.

Once again, I got to see the human brain and the interior surface of a human skull. A few feet farther away when fired and the damage would have catastrophic. It is a miracle I don't have nightmares about some of the things I saw there.

Punji Stakes

We patrolled one of the valley's deserted farm areas in the highlands when we came across the only punji stakes I saw in Vietnam. The enemy used the punji stakes to inflict lingering injuries on our soldiers or to restrict our movements. It tied up at least two more soldiers to carry an injured soldier until a medevac helicopter evacuated him.

Punji stakes are bamboo sticks a foot and a half to two feet long and roughly the width of a No. 2 pencil. The enemy dried them to make the stakes rigid then they sharpened one end to a point and fire hardened them. To compound their effect, the enemy frequently coated the points of their punji stakes with a material sure to cause infection. The most available material for the enemy was human excrement. The last step was embedding the blunt end in the soil in an area suitable to concealing them, usually knee to waist high grasses.

A punji stake is capable of inflicting a serious injury on those who do not pay attention to their surroundings. All were emplaced at the same angle and pointed in the same direction. This way they blended into the dry grasses and made them nearly impossible to see until one was upon them. This was the enemy's goal. Their sharp points could penetrate the unwary soldier's uniform and flesh.

They were emplaced at an ambush site to injure soldiers maneuvering out of the ambush or to force them to move in a different and more deadly direction.

We happened to approach the punji stakes from their rear. Because the stakes pointed away from us, it was easy to see them. I took a few minutes to examine the site and the stakes. Once I learned all I could, we destroyed the trap by simply stepping on them where they entered the ground. The job took only a few minutes.

Taking a Break at the Coconut Grove

Another day we came upon a small grove of coconut palm trees. Dozens of coconuts, still in their husks, lay on the ground. We stopped to investigate. I put out pickets as an early warning system of an enemy's approach. I rotated them to give every man an opportunity to enjoy a coconut. We split open the coconuts to eat some of the "coconut meat" and drink their "milk," a much-appreciated change in our regular diet of C-rations in the field.

I noticed the milk possessed a slight effervescence but did not give it much thought beyond hoping it had not gone bad. I liked the coconut milk; I drank about sixteen ounces of it while eating some of the coconut meat. We finished with the coconuts in fifteen to twenty minutes and continued patrolling.

Part Two—The 173rd Airborne Brigade

An hour later, I developed a headache mysteriously like the kind that accompanies a hangover. It suddenly dawned on me the effervescence meant the coconut milk had fermented into a mild alcoholic beverage. The headache quickly passed. Luckily, no one became noticeably intoxicated. I learned making moonshine was not a career choice for me.

13

Patrolling Deep
in the Central Highlands

C Company Replaces a South Vietnamese Battalion

We patrolled around Pleiku for a month or so. That ended when C Company was given the mission to temporarily replace a South Vietnamese Army battalion pulled out of its AO to support another South Vietnamese unit engaged in combat elsewhere. Let me be specific: C Company, an understrength Infantry company, with a field strength of about one hundred twenty veteran paratroopers, was to patrol an area which had required a South Vietnamese battalion, of probably four to five hundred Vietnamese soldiers, to patrol.

The men of "C" Company were experienced soldiers. They made little noise in the jungle or forests. Months of patrolling had worked out the squeaks and rattling in our web gear and rucksacks. The men didn't engage in idle chatter for two simple reasons: (1) they had nothing worth discussing in the jungle and (2) the jungle quiet makes voices audible over a great distance. Making noise can get you killed.

Helicopters flew us to the new AO. Our company commander informed us he intended the platoons to patrol independently. There was no other effective means to cover that much ground with our limited number of men. This meant the platoons might find themselves separated by two to three kilometers at times. This put us at some risk of being "defeated in detail" which means a smart enemy commander would attack the platoons one by one rather than seeking to attack C Company as a whole.

145

Part Two—The 173rd Airborne Brigade

I enjoyed the freedom of action. In the words of Mel Brooks, "It's good to be the King" even if you're only a small king in the middle of nowhere.

The battalion assigned one 4.2-inch (107mm) mortar and its crew to accompany us to provide indirect fire support. I trained on this powerful and versatile weapon while getting my commission but not enough to make me a mortar crewman. Like all mortars, it is accurate at close ranges but more of an area weapon at longer ranges, not a pinpoint weapon like artillery.

It's typically used against soft targets like enemy troops, trucks, and the kind of fortifications I'd seen with the 3rd Brigade. Its maximum range is a little more than 6,800 meters (four miles). Adjusting the aim through several firings is often necessary to achieve the best effect at the longer ranges.

We had artillery support as well, a battery of four 175 mm (about 6.9 inches) self-propelled guns. Each long-barreled gun is mounted on a tank chassis. Their maximum effective range is 32,000 meters (21 miles). They could be a bit erratic at their maximum range due to infinitesimal play in the weapon's long barrel or poor maintenance.

One must never overlook this last point when near the maximum range of supporting mortar or artillery fire. Many factors can cause their projectiles to hit as much as 100 meters (109 yards) from the target. It's best to get down.

The land we focused most of our patrols on lay around the hills with a base elevation approximately 700 meters (765 yards) above sea level. The average elevation of the hilltops was 800 to 900 meters (875 yards to 984 yards) above sea level.

From our perspective, the actual height of the hills was a mere hundred to two hundred meters (109 to 218 yards). These are usually surmountable but the thick brush and trees made it difficult to climb them with the loads we carried, especially in bad weather or if someone happened to be shooting at us. This thought went through my mind several times a day.

Patrolling this terrain gave me the opportunity to enhance my land navigation skills in the highlands. Luckily, I got a lot of practice while we patrolled for weeks without sighting any enemy forces or signs of their presence.

Our nights included ambushes, generally three squad-sized ambushes along one of the trails in my area per night or someplace we might find the enemy moving at night, which we didn't. The squads on the ends of our line of ambushes were to notify me when they sighted an enemy force coming into view or earshot. They were not to attack unless I authorized it. I wanted to be sure no larger enemy force followed behind a small advance party.

I also wanted to get the maximum effect when the center squad triggered the ambush. The job of the end squads was to close the door on any escaping enemy forces.

I knew my men were capable of defeating a force comparable in size to ours in a surprise attack but a larger unit, particularly a significantly larger one would create a situation calling for hit and run tactics, emphasis on the run.

I usually stayed with the central ambush. I would give the order to trigger the ambush when the enemy force reached us. This never happened. The outlying squads had a secondary job of preventing other enemy forces from coming to the aid of their ambushed comrades or staging a counterattack against us. A third option was to reinforce the central ambush or provide covering fire for the men withdrawing from an ambush that had backfired on us.

One thing about working in the Central Highlands is you spent a lot of time on hillsides or mountainsides. The steepness of the slopes varied. The steeper slopes made movement more difficult and tended to cause rain runoff to soak us when we stopped to rest from patrolling for a few minutes or to eat. Heavy rains made heating our C-rations extremely difficult but they are edible when cold. We found ways to heat our rations in inclement weather and rarely ate cold food.

What the rain did to us while we sat or slept on the ground was worse. Imagine spending days on end alternating between being wet and soaking wet. That is what we suffered during the rainy season in the highlands. Still, those incredible paratroopers did their jobs and

147

did them well. I learned this simple lesson about rain; once you are soaking wet you can't get any wetter.

I acquired an Army issue hammock somehow. I think I traded for it, or bought it from a soldier going home. I know I didn't steal it. I rigged it as a part of my rucksack's bedroll with my poncho liner a light quick dry "blanket" inside the hammock, which was inside my poncho. The poncho, being waterproof, kept the contents dry. It worked surprisingly well.

I could set up the hammock without unrolling it in three to five minutes, if I had the right size and appropriately spaced trees nearby. I tied the hammock tightly to the trees about two feet above the ground with the rope on each end. Then it was a simple matter to tie the cords on the corners of the poncho to small trees next to it. These converted the waterproof poncho into a tent. When turned broadside to the wind, the poncho kept most of the rain off me. Otherwise, I slept wet on the ground if it rained.

I was still wet in the hammock but slept warm inside the poncho liner. Best of all, my rucksack rested on its frame underneath the hammock. This kept the rucksack's contents out of the runoff water to the extent possible. My rifle sat on top of the rucksack, dry and close at hand in an emergency.

At this stage of the war, the military played a political numbers game with ambushes. All the Infantry units in the field had to report using the maximum number of ambushes possible. A bean counter sitting somewhere in the bowels of the Pentagon could provide his superiors with the prior night's number of ambushes. They, in turn, could impress the nation's political leadership and the public with how well the war was being fought. All of them would keep their jobs.

It didn't matter to them that I had less than thirty men instead of the forty-four the Table of Organization and Equipment ("T, O and E") authorized. It didn't matter that my men and I were kilometers from the nearest ground support. It didn't matter that I had minimal artillery and mortar support and was at the maximum ranges for those weapons. I played the game, usually, but I kept my squads close, no more than four or five hundred meters apart in open terrain, closer in terrain thick with brush, trees or jungle.

On rare occasions, when I felt it tactically unwise to split my already understrength platoon, I kept us together in one ambush. I simply made up the other two ambushes at nearby map coordinates. We made radio calls as if we had three ambushes. I have no doubt my CO knew this and would have done the same if our positions were reversed, probably had when he led a platoon. He never asked. Everybody was happy, even the bean counter.

The Elephant Incursion

One night two of the ambushes did not go as planned. The first thing to go wrong happened with the central ambush. We'd settled in place to wait in the tree line next to a trail bordering a large expanse of grassland. By large, I mean larger than the size of the largest football stadiums and their parking lots.

Late, but not yet midnight, the sudden and large explosion of a Claymore mine detonating happened at the front of the ambush. Dead silence followed. No one screamed in agony from grievous wounds. No one shot at us. I heard only silence.

It seemed the squad's sergeant had heard something rustling in the grass near our front. Fearing the enemy was trying to infiltrate our position, he detonated one of the Claymores emplaced along our front. Only no enemy existed, which a check in the morning proved. The noise was probably some kind of rodent rustling in the grass and leaves.

I simply looked at him and said, in a matter-of-fact whisper, "Blew your bush, didn't you?" A leader must appear unfazed no matter what the situation. It gives your men confidence in the leader and tends to prevent panic. It really does.

It was far too late to move to another site. I could not withdraw the center unit of a linear ambush without leaving the other squads without mutual support. Consequently, we stayed on a heightened alert status for the rest of the night. Because of that loud explosion, I didn't think any of the enemy would stop by. Still, losing a little sleep on high alert is a small price to pay to keep breathing.

Three or so hours before dawn, I heard a loud racket from the ambush to my left. It went on for about ten seconds. The racket consisted of yelling accompanied by the sounds of brush and tree limbs being thrashed and broken. It sounded like some sort of fight but I couldn't make sense of it. Then it subsided.

Minutes later, the racket began again with the same sounds. This time it stopped momentarily when a loud explosion took place followed by louder sounds of more brush and trees snapping. These sounds rapidly dwindled into the distance and faded away.

I radioed them for a Situation Report (SITREP). The squad leader responded immediately saying something big had tried to enter their position, but a grenade had scared it off. He told me everyone was all right.

The question in my mind was, "If not an enemy force what was it?" I was worried because tigers were known to roam the highlands. The big cats require a lot of food. I had not heard anything sounding like one of those big cats. I listened for a while to see if anything made a sound pointing to an enemy force moving around or toward us. I heard nothing.

When daylight arrived, I told the squad to my right to move to my location. The two squads and I marched to the position of the left-hand ambush to collect the third squad and to see what happened during the night. The squad sergeant told me it was an elephant that tried to enter the ambush site.

I had no doubt he was correct. The animal's footprints proved it. The most incredible part of the story was the elephant-sized tunnel, floored with crushed brush and broken saplings, the elephant had bored through the forest of saplings while making its escape. Only a mighty scared elephant, moving as fast as it could go, could have made that tunnel. Unbelievable? Yes, but the absolute truth nonetheless.

14

To Climb
a Mile High Mountain

June 1969

The Calm Before a Wave of Intense Activity Broke Over Us

Days passed with no enemy activity or sightings, so I changed tactics to move through the jungle on the lower hills a little quicker. I was hoping to come across recent signs of an enemy presence. We'd seen none to date.

I usually walked about the third or fourth man back in the line so I could make sure we followed the course I set and to see what lay ahead of us. That day, at one particular moment, I walked further back in the column to make it easier for my men to see me going about my job checking on things and to see the outward signs of their morale. From there my men also had an opportunity to ask me any important questions about our mission or destination, questions I wanted to ask during my own training.

My Infantry officer training involved a number of day and night marches. The night marches are the worst, not because of the dark but because not knowing our mission or destination is downright scary, especially in a combat situation. Both are bad for morale and combat effectiveness.

When I changed my position in the file from time to time to walk among my men during the marches, I did so with a purpose.

I intended to demonstrate my confidence in them and be seen doing my job. Ultimately, I sought to relieve any anxiety caused by not knowing critical information. This often triggers fear, particularly when you add in dense jungle or forest or no nearby supporting units. Fear makes men panic and act stupidly. Any of these can make them or all of us dead.

One time when I cut in and out of line as we passed through some particularly dense jungle vegetation, I looked up at the paratrooper ahead of me. Imagine my surprise to see a bone-white human skull riding atop his rucksack, bobbing like a bobble head doll. You don't see this every day, even in Vietnam.

"Where did you get that," I asked. He said, "I got it one night when I dug up a grave near our ambush. I cleaned and polished it with my toothbrush and toothpaste."

I wondered if I needed to be concerned about that paratrooper's mental state. On the other hand, he was a good soldier. "Lose the skull," I said. He did. I still wonder about his mental state.

The change was to stop using a single line. I reasoned I could cover a wider area in less time by establishing my command post, consisting of my platoon sergeant, my radio operator, medic, one squad, and me, in a defensible position. I had the other two squads drop their rucksacks at the command post. This gave them greater freedom of action and speed. With their loads pared down, I sent them out in a cloverleaf pattern to investigate the two to three hundred meters further along our line of march and the same distance to either side. The squad that stayed with me was my reserve force, if needed.

When the squads returned, I moved my command post to another location and repeated the procedure. I rotated the squads to give each squad a chance for an extended rest period. This allowed me to patrol a wider swath of terrain than was possible to achieve with a single line of march, and do it fairly quickly but only in a mostly open area. It works as well in dense jungle and forest.

A Dash Through the Jungle

Two of the squads had just moved out to perform their cloverleaf patrols when I received a radio call from my CO. He gave me orders to move to specific map coordinates, be there by a specified time, and establish a Pickup Zone (PZ) for four helicopters. My men and I were to board them. He gave me no more information, like why. Since the helicopters were already on the way, I needed to get busy planning my route. I recalled my squads.

Navigating accurately through various types of terrain, vegetation and weather using only a map and compass is a challenge, one I'd readily accepted. I actually enjoyed it.

My recalled squads returned in fifteen minutes, I used the time to identify the location of the PZ on the map and the compass direction to get there. I memorized the topography and likely vegetation I would encounter along the two kilometers (1.2 miles) straight line route I intended to take.

I believed a plan existed which explained this move, but no one shared such a plan with my Company CO or me. This surprised me because knowledge of what headquarters expected my men and me to accomplish is the mission. It's absolutely critical information in planning for what we might be walking into.

I never received orders such as these before or since that time. The lack of detail implied an attempt to surprise the enemy, or an unusual situation, or one that portended danger for my platoon. I didn't understand why only my one platoon got the orders. My CO said nothing to indicate what situation required such a rapid shift of just one platoon. I needed answers to a lot of questions.

I trusted my CO to tell me any intelligence received on the enemy situation, but I had to ask to be sure. I asked. He said he'd received nothing.

When the squads returned, I briefed my sergeants on our new orders, an easy task because of the paucity of details those orders contained. I added I intended to lead our column at a fast pace in a straight line across more than two kilometers of jungle-covered hills and cautioned them to keep their men close together to avoid losing anyone. We saddled up and off we went.

I set a fast pace. I didn't ignore the possible dangers to which I exposed my men and myself. But this time I wasn't overly concerned about them for the simple reason I was confident my "as the crow flies" route avoided trails the enemy used for medium and long-distance travel. As it turned out, it worked. We didn't come across a trail or any signs of the enemy.

I'd memorized the route on the map to avoid trails, specifically because the dense jungle was unlikely to hold any dangers of ambush or booby traps for us. We arrived at the PZ with a few minutes to spare, without a single casualty or losing a single man.

I told my platoon sergeant to divide the twenty-seven of us into four approximately equal sized groups to correspond to the number of arriving helicopters. The sergeants positioned their men to board the helicopters once they arrived. The general rule is six soldiers per UH-1 helicopter. However, at the end of the winter rainy season, the air was cooler and denser, meaning a UH-1 would gain the additional lift needed to carry seven men. All of us could board the helicopters but with little room to spare. The sergeants positioned their men to board the helicopters on arrival.

When the co-pilot radioed for us to mark the PZ, I gave one of my men a smoke grenade and told him to toss it on the PZ. I ordered the first paratrooper in each line to raise his rifle high over his head to mark where we hoped each helicopter would land. I say hoped because although my platoon sergeant placed the four groups far enough apart for the helicopters to land safely, experience also taught us the value of flexibility. The helicopters landed on time.

Hope may spring eternal, but helicopter pilots have their own version of hope. I estimate that in only one out of three pickups will the helicopters actually land where the Infantry hoped. As usual, we needed to run to each helicopter. We did it this time too, once the helicopters settled to the ground. We boarded quickly and in two minutes found ourselves flying over the jungle to an unknown destination for an unknown mission.

One UH-1 Turns Back; No One Knows
Where We're Going

The helicopter's crew chief yelled in my ear about five minutes into the flight. He shared the news that one of the helicopters was having some sort of mechanical trouble and needed to return my men to the PZ to await another helicopter.

Seven of my men were left alone in the middle of nowhere waiting for another helicopter to pick them up. I knew their danger but lacked the power to do anything. This was an inauspicious beginning. It soon got worse.

The crew chief yelled in my ear again after another fifteen minutes of flying. "The pilot wants to talk to you."

I took the radio handset from my radio operator; it was still tuned to the air-ground frequency.

The pilot asked, "Where are you going?" I answered, "I don't know. Don't you?" He didn't.

I didn't know the starting point for my mission on the ground or my objective, another disquieting aspect of our mission. We flew around in wide circles for the next half hour before another helicopter with my missing men joined the circling. We had four UH-1 helicopters boring holes in the sky. Why?

Eventually, I spotted a lone helicopter in the distance headed our way. Someone in it tossed a smoke grenade onto a small flat section on the lower portion of a narrow mountain ridge.

Our new LZ was only big enough to accept one helicopter at a time. Each helicopter set down only long enough for us to get out and move away. Once we cleared the far ends of the rotor blades, it lifted off to make room for the next one to land.

Fortunately, all of my men were there. Unfortunately, I had no idea where the new LZ was located on the map. Because of the circling, I had the wrong view and didn't get to look for the identifiable topography around the LZ. Once we landed, I got busy getting my bearings. I figured out my location pretty quickly.

We stood less than halfway up the side of a mountain my maps showed as 1,720 meters (1.07 miles) above sea level.

I radioed my company commander for orders immediately after determining my location. "Battalion hasn't shared the mission with me," he said, which left me twisting in the wind.

I, and my understrength platoon, had landed deep in "Injun Country" and far from the rest of "C" Company, our only source of Infantry support. To my way of thinking, this marked a seriously screwed up operation.

I had to wait a while longer to find out the nature of my mission. We had enough time to eat a quick lunch. Napoleon had it right: "An army marches on its stomach." But I think he meant its logistics. We faced a possible uphill climb along a steep ridge to the unknown on the mountaintop. Best to eat first. I moved the platoon to a tree line at the lower edge of the LZ for concealment while we ate.

I waited for more information and orders. I did know one thing, the trail, which ran through the LZ, ran both uphill and downhill into dense foliage. In my heart I knew the mission involved heading uphill.

The Long Climb to an Enemy Basecamp in the Clouds

Without orders, I had to decide to go uphill or downhill. To wait longer, with the dangers multiple helicopter landings can bring, was not a viable choice. I opted for downhill, the easier of the two. It had a decided advantage; it closed the distance between my platoon and the rest of the company and its support if I needed it. Once my men finished eating, we set off down the mountain. We'd marched less than a hundred meters when my RTO said our CO wanted to speak with me. He gave me the mission.

My orders were to lead my platoon to the top of the mountain, scout the large enemy base camp known to be there, and see if any enemy troops occupied it. This is a traditional reconnaissance mission for an Infantry platoon. But let's recap the situation from my point of view so you can see what wasn't traditional about this mission.

I commanded an understrength rifle platoon of twenty-seven

combat veteran paratroopers while a fully manned platoon has forty-four. When we got to the top of the mountain, our separation from the rest of "C" Company would widen to at least eight-tenths of a kilometer (half a mile) vertically and between two and five and a half kilometers (1.2–3.5 miles) laterally from the other platoons. The vertical part consisted of an extremely steep sided and narrow mountain ridge leading to the top of the mountain. There's more.

When we arrived at the top of the mountain, we'd be at the maximum ranges of the single 4.2-inch mortar with the company and a 175 mm artillery battery. This was the totality of the fire support available to me. This was a danger also. Their accuracy was a bit dicey at their maximum ranges.

Last, but not least, the thick clouds enveloping the top of the mountain meant we had no air support of any kind. These clouds also prevented any illumination from the moon or the stars reaching us. We could look forward to an absolutely black night with not even the light from a single star to break the darkness.

Our position was under a triple canopy of trees, which means three layers of trees of different heights. To understand, picture a grove of avocado trees about 40 feet tall, towered over by pine trees 90 to 100 feet tall, towered over by some real giants 150 or more feet tall some of which looked to be about two meters wide at the base. The layers of tree leaves seeking the sun left only a sort of twilight at ground level during the day. It also meant we did not face dense brush at ground level. This is the only good point.

On these happy notes, we began the climb to the top of the mountain in the damp and gloom twilight of the triple canopy forest. Every inch of our way we tramped across wet hard-packed ground, wet rocks, and wet plants and wet leaves. The wet hard-packed ground was the worst because the nearly constant drizzle from the clouds made it slick. The wet leaves made it extremely slippery and nearly impossible to gain traction in some places.

Climbing with the weight of the arms and equipment we carried was a dangerous proposition at times. At times the climb resembled crawling. We clawed for handholds on tree roots or whatever came to hand to get up the one near vertical part of the trail or, in some instances, to keep from sliding backwards. We stopped only once to rest when the slope leveled out.

The Leeches Came

When we stopped to rest the leeches came at us. Of course, there were leeches; they lived in the dampness. They seemed to be everywhere. This day kept getting better and better!

The typical leech is about an inch to an inch and a half in length when empty. All of them looked empty! They came at me from all directions, moving by bunching their rear ends up to their front ends and rapidly extending their front ends forward to gain ground and repeat the movement. Their quick movements made it look like they were jumping towards us. I assumed they sensed our body heat.

It's a bit unnerving when first you see them jumping at you and even more unnerving when you discover one had attached itself to you and settled down to suck your blood.

The Army provided us with insect repellant. Serendipitously, it's the perfect weapon to protect us from the leeches because the high alcohol content in the insect repellant killed them instantly. I drew a six-foot wide circle around me with the insect repellant, which stopped the leeches from entering the circle. Then I shot any leeches inside the circle with the repellant.

I drenched my pant legs where they were tucked inside my boots with insect repellant to keep leeches from getting to my skin while I walked. I shared this idea with my men. I do not recall any of us having any more leech problems.

The light had faded a great deal by the time we reached a point about two to three hundred meters down slope from the base camp. It took us more than five hours to march, climb, crawl and pull ourselves up nearly a kilometer (three quarters of a mile) from our LZ to a few hundred meters shy of the mountaintop. The darkness was closing in on us. I ruled out the possibility of going any farther in the approaching absolute blackout conditions. In the waning minutes of daylight, I finally found a spot that offered some possibility of being a defensible position for my platoon. We set up a cold, dinnerless, lightless, and silent defensive position.

I'd already made up my mind not to set out ambushes that night. The situation posed too great a risk to my men. The ridge was too narrow and too steep sided for movement in a blackout, and lacked any suitable sites to set up ambushes. I asked to be relieved of the responsibility to set out ambushes. My CO gave me the only response permitted: No. I understood this. We all have our orders, which must be obeyed. I was expected to subject my platoon to the risk of piecemeal destruction in order for a bean counter and some politicians to sleep well.

This was another case of the Army having its policies and me having mine. Mine told me to keep my men out of harm's way. I didn't give a damn if the bean counters and the politicians didn't sleep well. They didn't make the climb to the mountaintop with us. I circled my platoon and settled in before it became pitch-black. I had two squads radio in SITREPS to me as if they were ambushes. I gave a set of false map coordinates for those pseudo ambushes. The tactical situation dictated this course of action.

I am certain my company CO knew what I did. He was a good and experienced commander who might have done the same if our positions were reversed. Probably had when he led a platoon. He didn't ask me and I didn't tell.

Our night position consisted of giant tree boles and a number of jeep-sized boulders. I worried about our situation once the sun had set and the pitch-blackness set in. I'm not talking about the low light level in a house at night. I mean absolutely black and lightless. The night lacked the weakest of lights to pierce that stygian darkness.

One of my men walked out of our perimeter to relieve himself. Because of the blackness he lost his way. He finally stumbled back into our position through blind luck. If his luck went the other way, stumbling over the edge of that narrow ridge, falling down a steep slope with scattered trees, and littered with boulders of various sizes was a distinct possibility for him. If that happened, I could do nothing until after learning the enemy situation at daybreak.

I radioed my CO with a request for harassing and interdiction

(H&I) fires on the base camp. He said, "No they'll just make them stay down in their holes and hide."

I told him, "I'm fine with that, the enemy can't attack us if they're in their holes." I did not get the H&I fires.

Being in absolute blackness is unnatural for humans. Having to fight for your life in absolute darkness makes it even more terrifying. Since I saw nothing good for us coming out of a fight in total blackness, I'm glad I ruled out risking combat that night and avoided needless casualties from enemy action, or friendly fire casualties, or injuries from falling down the steep sides of the mountain. The men sensed the seriousness of our situation. They were subdued, rarely speaking and then only in a whisper.

Fortunately, nothing happened during the night. This left only the coming morning and the base camp to deal with. I detected no sounds or smells coming from the top of the mountain during the night, which gave me hope.

Just before daylight, we waited for the first light of a weak dawn to break the absolute darkness. I waited until I could tell a white thread from a black one. I learned this from a movie but I don't recall which. It allegedly came from the Arabs. My recent research shows it is a way to tell the day from the night, which is what I did. It comes from the Quran 2:187.

Then I gave my sergeants the order to quietly saddle up. Because when marching to battle an Infantry officer's place is in front, I led my men the remaining two hundred yards up the steep knife-edge ridge that led to the base camp. We approached in a single file through misty clouds on a ridge too narrow to march with two men abreast.

As we followed the trail to the base camp, the clouds muffled all sounds creating a deathly quiet. I listened for the faintest sound ahead of me to give away the presence of an enemy force and tried to detect any odor of a human presence. I heard nothing. I smelled nothing. Their absence comforted me but only a little.

My fears we might walk into a cauldron eased a little as we approached closer. My senses detected nothing that pointed to the presence of an enemy force but my fear did not fade entirely.

The ground began to level out and widen when we neared the base camp. I motioned for the men to spread out a little. Through the weak predawn half-light, the mists of the clouds, and the dozens of saplings ahead of me, I barely made out a series of diagonal defensive trenches, which looked like a sergeant's chevrons cut down the middle by the trail. They were empty, which shortly proved true of the entire base camp. Mission accomplished with no casualties.

What I felt went beyond relief. A few alert enemy soldiers in the trenches and we could've had one hell of a firefight.

The trail widencd beyond the sparse undergrowth and saplings at the edge of the base camp. I saw not a soul, only a deserted oblong piece of flat ground. My men and I would live to see another day. I told my RTO to radio our CO, "The base camp is empty."

We spent an hour or so examining every inch of the camp without finding any signs of recent occupancy. The men found a few nondescript pieces of canvas but no weapons or ammunition and no equipment. The squad I sent to investigate the area a hundred meters beyond the far side of the camp returned empty handed. Even so I saw nothing to convince me the enemy had abandoned the camp. The chevrons-like trenches were in good repair.

After that, I told my sergeants to have their men eat their breakfasts and take care of personal needs. I saw their usually good mood return in their faces and heard it in their low voices. They also felt relieved to be alive. I doubt any one of them felt more relief about that than I.

We heard M-16 fire from the direction of the base of the mountain. Radio traffic said one of the other platoons moving closer to us came across two enemy soldiers fixing breakfast. They opened fire on them and missed. The enemy soldiers escaped and were last seen heading uphill in my direction. My CO told me to take a position to cut off their escape. I stretched my platoon along one hundred fifty meters of that trail along the knife-edge ridge. We waited for over an hour without hearing or seeing anyone. I doubted they tried to climb the steep slope.

The next day was a resupply day for the company, but I had no orders to come down from the mountain. Time continued to march while we scouted the top of the mountain and waited for the two enemy soldiers. It grew too late to go downhill in the coming blackness.

I moved my platoon several hundred meters farther down the ridge trail to a point with small trees. I set the men to cutting an LZ. We used the machetes we carried to chop them down and create an LZ wide and level enough to land a single helicopter. They nearly finished it by late afternoon. The finishing touches needed to wait until morning.

Their efforts pleased me in part because we were low on food. A few of the men had little in the way of rations so we pooled them, including the extra C-ration cans I found in the bottom of my rucksack. The cans accidentally accumulated over a long time. Their presence explained why my rucksack seemed unnecessarily heavy.

Four of us combined what we had to make a kind of communal meal. I created a chicken and rice casserole using a freeze-dried chicken and rice meal mixed with a C-ration can of chicken and noodles and small tins of cheese. It fed the four of us and was surprisingly good.

With dinner finished, I circled the wagons again. We spent an uneventful night in another platoon-sized ambush in the darkness.

My men finished the landing zone in the early morning of the next day. After its completion my CO told me the clouds still didn't permit a resupply helicopter to reach us. Instead, he ordered me to bring my platoon down the mountain to the resupply point where the rest of C Company gathered.

Since descending via the trail took hours, I abandoned any idea of using it. I led my men in a slide down the steep mountainside instead, a much quicker way too. We crouched and leaned back on our rucksacks to give us stable positions for the slide downhill. We went down much quicker this way. The unavoidable speed required each of us to focus to prevent gravity from doing to us what we worked so hard to avoid on the way up. Our descent resembled a controlled slide down a leaf-covered mountainside. The thick layer of dry leaves acted as a lubricant. I estimate our elapsed time for the slide at ten to fifteen minutes.

14. To Climb a Mile High Mountain

My second thoughts about sliding down proved unnecessary. I worried some of the men, myself included, might lose control of their speed or direction. Anyone who crashed into a tree or boulder risked catastrophic results. Worse from my perspective was the likelihood of us speeding away from the injured. I envisioned a climb up the steep mountainside to rescue him.

Miraculously each of us controlled his speed and, to a lesser extent, his course. No one crashed into a tree or boulder and we stayed together. We were filthy by the time we got down to the valley floor at the base of the mountain. I must say as a child I would have loved to slide down the mountainside repeatedly.

15

Resupply, Mail, a Desert and Bouncing Bettys

The resupply was disappointing if not unconscionable. Invariably a hot meal from the mess hall came with each resupply including this one, but most of it had been eaten by the time the 1st Platoon arrived. My disappointment that no one made any effort to save enough hot food to feed my men is understandable. I am not saying we missed a gourmet banquet but hot scrambled eggs and sausage mean a lot to men who eat out of a can most days.

A core part of our responsibility as commissioned officers is to take care of our men. It is second only to our duty to complete our missions. This is a large part of the reason the men willingly follow us into Tennyson's "valley of death," or, in my case, to that mountaintop enemy base camp. Someone's failure to ensure enough hot food would be left for my men breached that duty.

The mail came with the resupply. I'd extended my tour for another six months to get another special leave for a trip to Rio de Janeiro in August. I'd written home asking my family to send certain clothes and my large suitcase to me.

I receive two packages way too soon. One turned out to be a small suitcase without the clothes I had requested in it. The second contained the wrong military hat, the one we called the flying saucer because it was round. It lacked the large gold eagle that attaches to the front of it. The hat and the small suitcase were useless. I could not carry them around with me and the helicopter had left. I wore the hat and carried the empty suitcase for a while purely for laughs. I burned them before heading back into the nearby forest.

A Bamboo Viper vs. Peaches

We patrolled the area a while longer with little of note occurring with one exception. My platoon and I came across a somewhat level piece of ground on a slope in a forest. I halted the platoon there for lunch.

After my lunch, I sat on a tree stump in the warmth of some sunlight while eating a can of peaches. The scarcity of direct sunlight in the jungles and forests of the highlands coupled with the scarcity of peaches in C-rations made this a special moment. I had barely begun to eat the peaches when I noticed a bamboo viper, about two and a half feet long, slowly gliding between my boots. Its color was the green of young bamboo leaves. Its head had the classic arrowhead shape of vipers. Decades later I learned it was an adult.

I didn't see any way to move away from it which didn't involve startling it into striking me or losing the peaches or both. I figured I could safely flip over backward and avoid being bitten. But doing that meant losing the peaches.

I let my curiosity get the better of me. I sat still and watched the bamboo viper's slow passage between my boots because peaches are sufficiently uncommon to accept the risk of the snake biting me. It's called having priorities. I finished the peaches while the viper slowly slithered away from me. I stood up and casually walked away to alert my men to its presence.

We continued patrolling for a number of weeks of the same routine. We alternated between climbing hills and marching through the valleys but never encountered any enemy forces. The base camp on the mountaintop and the two that got away were the only signs of an enemy presence the company encountered. Unsurprising given the great expanse and the rugged terrain of the Central Highlands. Finally, we received orders to return to Pleiku. We flew back in groups.

We patrolled around Pleiku for another month without meeting any enemy forces. One day we received maps of a new AO. The company boarded some helicopters for another special mission, so frequent an event that years earlier the paratroopers of 173rd Brigade commonly referred to themselves as gypsies because of their constant movement around South Vietnam. Little did I know we were about to see Vietnam's most unusual piece of terrain. It took me by surprise.

A Singular Terrain for Vietnam

Late July 1969

In mid–July, "C" Company's new orders required us to move to a new AO. We flew a moderately great distance for a UH-1 helicopter. I don't know where to find this AO on a map of South Vietnam. Like all topographic maps, mine only covered a specific area and did not contain any habitations large enough to be on a nationwide map.

The helicopters landed us in a landscape with two striking aspects, a moderately high temperature and bone-dry conditions. We landed in a desert!

The surface of the desert floor consisted of a mixture of sand or fine soil and small pebbles and scattered small knolls. As in all deserts, vegetation was nearly nonexistent. What vegetation we found were scattered clumps of dried grasses and stunted trees on each irregularly shaped knoll, which had diameters of approximately thirty feet. I saw no ground cover of any kind anywhere.

Nearby low stone canyons and other rock formations bore the ages-old signs of shaping by free-flowing water. Nothing pointed to any recent rain having fallen there. Of all the terrains and vegetation types in Vietnam, this one alone gave me a sense of home. I could have been standing in one of southern California's high deserts.

"Bouncing Betty" Mines

I led my platoon over one of those pitifully small knolls with a stunted tree. I noticed hundreds of metallic objects scattered widely on the slopes of the knoll and the surrounding desert floor. Their coloring and shapes tended to blend into the knoll's coloring. They looked like gray Master Locks with a black wing in the shape of an inverted "V" on each shoulder. I remember thinking the wing's purpose was to slow the speed of each falling device. The top of each "lock" had a well in which set a silver-grey ball, smaller than a golf ball and larger than a quarter. Not all of them mind you, simply most!

The absence of about twenty percent of the balls triggered an old memory and galvanized me into action. My men and I stood on a knoll covered with numerous airdropped United States anti-personnel mines. The black wings didn't slow the fall of those devices; they triggered them when disturbed!

I immediately "froze" the platoon. I let them know we stood in a minefield and described the mines.

These were the modern-day equivalents of the "Bouncing Betty" mines of World War II infamy. Those balls being the "Bouncing" part. When triggered each "bounces" to waist height and detonates. They didn't kill; they maimed! They were intended to inflict a number of horrible nonlethal injuries on the person who triggered it, or anyone nearby, including injuries to the genitals, abdomen or face and eyes.

A second purpose of this type of mine is to require other soldiers to come to the aid of the wounded soldier and evacuate him from the area. The idea is to remove as many enemy soldiers as possible from the battle.

A third purpose is to bar an enemy's movements. It seemed a waste of ordnance on that small knoll. Backyard swimming pools are bigger than each of the knolls. Each was only six feet above the desert floor. Only on schoolyards do boys fight for possession of a six-foot hill.

These mines are clearly visible as soon as you look for them. Once seen, it was easy to very carefully step around them. I told my men to look around them and locate the mines closest to them, particularly those with their silver-grey balls still in place.

I cautioned my men to watch where they stepped. When I believed my men completely knew the situation, I led them out of the minefield. No one triggered a mine. No one was injured. My men were the only ones in the company to encounter the mines.

I radioed my situation to my company commander with a description of the devices. I also shared my anger that none of us, including him, received any warning of their presence.

These devices come in large canisters which the U.S. Air Force drops like bombs. They are set to "explode" low above the ground to obtain maximum dispersion of the mines. I also believe the wings may have acted to slow the mine's rate of descent to avoid them triggering on impact. This defeats their intended purpose.

This type of landmine is particularly nasty from my point of view, effective but nasty. The first problem is the lack of notice of the presence of the mines or their extent. The fact they are airdropped means some of them probably fell far outside the intended area for their emplacement. Alternatively, and my choice, a pilot dropped the canister containing the mines to avoid the paperwork of returning it to the airbase.

The lack of a prior warning of their presence angered me, not their presence. Any one of my men could have been horribly maimed because of the lack of warning. My men's good luck continued; the desert environment lacked the undergrowth to completely hide the presence of the mines.

We took a short break on another knoll which looked much like the first one but with a little more scrub brush and a few stunted trees that offered a little shade, and it had none of those mines on or around it. While there, I caught sight of one of the denizens of that desert. At five inches long and as wide as my ring finger, it was one of the largest centipedes I've ever seen. It crawled on a tree limb quite close to me. Discretion being the better part of valor, I relocated myself to a place a short distance away.

I received orders to join my company commander. His coordinates put him about a kilometer away. The ground changed to sand as I neared his location. What appeared to be merely a stone formation near his position turned out to be exterior surface of a canyon wall rising up about forty feet. It reminded me of the water-worn formations in the Grand Canyon or of similar locations in the southwestern United States. Millions of years of running water or wind-blown sand smoothed the canyon's walls.

I only took one semester of geology in college four years later, which does not make me a geologist. The uniform depth of the sand floors and the smoothness of the canyon walls resulted from sand-laden running water as it cut down through stone over millions of years. This was a very old desert.

A Special Leave in Rio de Janeiro

20 July 1969 to 4 September 1969

My CO called me to his position to discuss my thirty-day special leave which came with my latest six-month extension of my tour of duty in Vietnam. I intended to go to Rio de Janeiro because of its reputation as an international playground. I'd set the special leave for the early part of August. But first I needed to get a passport. My CO told me he intended to send me to the rear a few days early to give me the time I needed to get a passport from the United States Embassy in Saigon. I left a few days later but not before an unusual experience.

"C" Company's patrolling took us near a U.S. military installation, whose name I don't recall. Its presence was a pleasant surprise. The men got a chance for a partial day's rest and to use its PX. This PX was essentially a small full-service department store, which included an FTD florist shop. I'd done some traveling in Saigon and hadn't seen one there. Perhaps this was the only FTD florist shop in Vietnam. Nonetheless, finding it was a fortuitous event.

My mother had the only August birthday in my immediate family. I took advantage of the opportunity to send her flowers for her birthday as a surprise. I heard the fact I found a way to send the flowers astonished and pleased her. I never told her how I accomplished this feat.

A helicopter flew me to the battalion's headquarters on our next resupply day. There I received my travel orders for my special leave, which contained a provision for me to go to the embassy in Saigon to get my passport. This worked out quite well; my departure airport for the trip to Rio de Janeiro, via Southern California and Miami, was Tan Son Nhut Air Base outside of Saigon. I caught a U.S. Air Force C-130 transport at the airstrip at brigade headquarters for the trip to Tan Son Nhut to Air Force Base. I never saw the Central Highlands again.

Getting the passport took a couple of days. First, I had to get a passport photo, easily done in Saigon. I did this on the day I arrived there. I turned it in to the embassy along with my application for a passport. The clerk told me to come back in two days to pick up the passport. The embassy issued my passport on July 23, 1969. I scheduled a seat on the next military flight from Tan Son Nhut to Travis Air Force Base near San Francisco.

I noticed an Army physician in the terminal. By the look of him, he was new to the Army. I quietly and respectfully pointed out the incorrect placement of his Captain and Medical Corps insignia. I suggested it might draw laughter from other members of the Army in the terminal. He confirmed he was a physician and new to the Army. I changed the insignia to the proper display and explained how to get to his unit.

He thanked me and we parted, he to save lives and me to have the time of my life. My flight announced it was boarding passengers a short while later for the first leg of the trip to Brazil.

I arrived at Travis Air Force Base. From there I caught a shuttle to San Francisco International Airport. There I used my travel orders to schedule a flight to Rio de Janeiro through John Wayne Airport in Orange County and Miami's International Airport. I needed to pick up my Class A uniform, the green one which looked a little like a business suit, and some of my civilian clothes and a suitcase from my home in Orange County, California. For whatever reason, the anti-war crowd left me alone.

I needed my Class A uniform because I'd found I received better treatment that way when I traveled. I would wear the uniform on the airline flights and the civilian clothes in Brazil.

The nonstop flight on National Airlines from Los Angeles

International Airport to the airport in Miami was the airline and route that saw the most hijackings to Cuba. I landed in Miami without incident. The first thing I did was get a nice room at the Fontainebleau Hotel in Miami. I did not sleep well in their bed. It was too soft. I guess I'd become used to sleeping on the ground or in a hammock.

My flight to Rio did not leave until the next morning. This left me with some time to kill. Since I was a member, I took a taxi to the Miami Playboy Club. I intended to spend some of the afternoon there. A couple of well-off businessmen and I were the only patrons in the Club. We talked about the war, life and who knows what. It was an enjoyable couple of hours. They bought most of the drinks. I didn't drink too many. After a few hours and still sober, I returned to the hotel to get some rest before the next day's flight.

The next morning, I boarded a Pan Am Boeing 707 for the first leg of my round-trip travel to Rio de Janeiro. It departed the Miami airport as scheduled for the long nonstop flight. The stewardesses took good care of me, nothing out of the ordinary, and respected my long sleeping periods. An infantryman in combat takes his sleep where and when he can. I was trying to catch up, which is a physiological impossibility. The flight landed at Rio de Janeiro on August 5, 1969.

I made the U.S. Embassy my first stop, after clearing customs. I needed to check in with the Military Attaché's office to get my orders stamped to prove I came to Rio and get some tips and some advice about the city. The tip was where to find the better hotels. The advice was not to wear my uniform in public. American servicemen had been attacked while wearing their uniforms in Rio de Janeiro. All good to know.

I walked the streets of Saigon many times with no problems with the Vietnamese. Now I must worry about Brazilians attacking me in Rio de Janeiro. Our world is a truly strange place.

I got a nice room at a good hotel on Copacabana Beach. My room's location on the fifth floor, while not palatial, was nonetheless clean, well maintained, and comfortable. Best of all the bed had a firm mattress. I slept soundly.

My room's balcony faced directly onto Copacabana Beach across the street, giving me spectacular views up and down the beach. This balcony was large enough to accommodate a small dining table with two chairs plus two lounge chairs. I ate a magnificent breakfast there every morning. While I dined, I watched the few women in bikinis sunbathing on the beach. I'm a guy; deal with it. It turned out it was winter in Rio de Janeiro. The temperature stayed at a comfortable eighty degrees Fahrenheit with a sea breeze. The skies were blue. Life was good.

On the nights when I was not tired from the day's tourist activities, I went to discos. I kept the Attaché's advice in mind and wore only civilian clothes. I couldn't disguise the military haircut but nothing ever happened to me. I did not get drunk, and I behaved myself. I enjoyed myself without creating a problem.

The days I spent on foot exploring the life of the city. I tried to understand Brazil's currency, which is not easy due to the Brazilian Government's revaluation of its currency. It began as a cure for the devaluation of the nation's currency during serious inflation problems. Now its currency was undergoing revaluation.

To save money, Brazil didn't withdraw their currency from circulation and issue new bills. The banks simply stamped the bills with a new value and put them back into circulation, which made it difficult to calculate the prices of things. I gave up; I put down the cash and collected the change.

One day, instead of walking about the city, I hired a taxi for the day to take me sightseeing throughout the city. It cost only twenty dollars; money well spent.

I saw more of the city, including the slums on the hillsides immediately behind the city, a very depressing sight. A more depressing sight was seeing the poor Brazilians, including many children, scrambling over the tremendous mounds of trash, which lay adjacent to the slums. All searched for anything which could be sold for the cash needed to buy food.

We drove up to the gigantic statue of Jesus Christ on Corcovado Mountain, a truly impressive work. A number of street vendors stood around on the mountaintop selling gemstones. Brazil has a number of precious and semi-precious stones among its resources.

Street vendors sold them for a pittance because of the great amounts of them their mines produced. For three dollars, I bought a necklace of eighteen rough polished robin's egg sized amethyst stones held together with silver wire. I later found out one similar to it sold for twenty-five times this in the United States. I also bought tourmaline and aquamarine semi-precious gems in several carats each for less than a hundred dollars and possibly similar savings over U.S. prices. I do not know if they are quality gems. I gave the aquamarine to my sister and the tourmaline to my mother.

The trip continued by taking a long drive through the hills and mountains behind Rio de Janeiro to the coast south of the city, an incredibly picturesque drive through beautiful hills and valleys. Near sea level, we passed a small grotto with a waterfall and pool of water. Like the tea plantation in the Central Highlands of Vietnam, I remember the tranquility and the beauty of this grotto.

The trees surrounding the grotto shaded much of it. The shade probably kept it cool, even on the hot days. Only enough direct sunlight penetrated to create flashes of light from the waterfall and the small waves where the waterfall plunged into the pool.

Finally, we came to sea level on the coast highway somewhere between Rio de Janeiro and Sao Paulo. I saw not a single manmade thing on the pristine beach or along the coast highway in sight in either direction. Remember this was 1969. We returned to the city where I continued my nighttime adventures.

I left Rio de Janeiro on August 14, 1969. There is only so much you can do when you travel by yourself. I used the remainder of my leave to see my family and the friends I could find. They expressed their concern because I had signed up for another six months in Vietnam. They felt I was pushing my luck.

I included this trip as it was only possible because of the Vietnam War. I believe not many Infantry men took advantage of it because at the end they had to return to the war.

I returned to Vietnam a little over a month after I departed. The travel time did not count as part of the leave. It didn't start until I arrived in Rio de Janeiro and I had my orders stamped with the date I arrived at the U.S. Embassy there. I returned to Vietnam for the next to last time. The last time was when I returned from R&R in Hawaii, which also came with my extension.

I stopped at brigade headquarters to secure transportation to the 3rd Battalion in Pleiku. I discovered the entire 3rd Battalion had been shifted to a new AO. It felt a little like coming home from school and finding your family had moved.

16

Pacification, Stupid Questions and a Heavy Machine Gun

---

17 September 1969 to 9 March 1970

Back to LZ Uplift

The 3rd Battalion had been relocated to LZ Uplift to replace the 1st Battalion. The 1st Battalion had been sent to somewhere in the highlands; I never did learn exactly where or why. These are questions about which I did not need to concern myself until it became important, I know. I had too much to concern me in leading the 1st Platoon of C Company to worry about the 1st Battalion.

My arrival at C Company's new rear area at LZ Uplift, on or about 4 September 1969, came with a sort of *déjà vu* aspect to it. Nothing had changed, well almost nothing. Except for the 1st Battalion the same units remained based there. The helicopter refueling and rearming point still remained a central feature.

The big news was LZ Uplift possessed a steak house! Many times, the steak house would be a lifesaver for me, but that was some months away.

I reported for duty with C Company. The first thing I heard was they thought I was not coming back. I never understood why they thought this because they knew my special leave orders required me to return. Then came the bad news. Because of my seniority over the other lieutenants, I had been made the company's new Executive Officer (XO). I did not want the job.

My CO's decision made sense. I would promote to captain on

November 19, a little over two months away. An Infantry company has but one captain. The promotion necessitated my transfer out of C Company. In the meantime, logic dictated I, with my experience, must become the XO while the new officer began learning what is required of an Infantry platoon leader in combat operations.

A rookie first lieutenant fresh out of the Infantry training which follows ROTC (Reserve Officer Training Corps) now led the 1st Platoon. A green college kid commanding my platoon was unthinkable to me. I'd conveniently forgotten my greater greenness as a rookie second lieutenant when I took command of my first platoon.

My CO came in from the field to speak with me about my role with the company and my future with the Army. I explained I was a combat commander, not a desk jockey. I added I had no intention of staying for a career in the Army. This meant I did not need my record to show I served as a company level executive officer. But the new lieutenant's career needed to show service as a company executive officer.

I liked and respected my company commander; I did not play any games with him. I simply asked for my platoon back. I made sure he knew he could count on me to do an excellent job as his executive officer if he put me in the position. I really did nothing more than express my feelings. I got my platoon back. My CO made the arrangements. I had to spend a few days with the new lieutenant showing me around the AO and village the 1st Platoon protected.

Pacification September 1969

C Company had entered into the pacification business. The 1st Platoon was charged with protecting one of the larger villages in the company's AO. It happened to lie by a medium-sized shallow inland bay. The bay was connected to the ocean by a very narrow inlet. I never saw any boats transiting the inlet or on the waters of the bay.

The orientation of the village was on a north to south axis. It had dimensions of about one hundred fifty meters in length and a width equivalent to a little more than two thatched huts, or hooches as we called them, about thirty feet at its widest point. The northern portion of the village was deserted.

An open kilometer of sand ran from the coast to the east side of the village. This kilometer of sand was really a deep beach. Where it ended by the village, it was a forty-foot sand dune with about a fifty-degree slope. It was separated from the village by a small pond of water of questionable drinkability; I never saw any villager draw water from it. Fortunately, they did have a fresh water well which we used without contracting any illnesses.

The VC had forced the villagers with home sites on the northern end of the village to move to the top of that sand dune. They planted an unknown number of the Claymore mines they took from that beached landing craft, as booby-traps to deter U.S. and South Vietnamese Forces from entering. Shortly after I returned, Army engineers attempted to get rid of the mines with Bangalore torpedoes but with only limited success.

Most of the time I ran squad sized patrols during the daylight hours to keep the VC off balance or catch them on the open sand. The area was smaller than the one I had west of Saigon. I went with one of these. This is how I saw the still beached and empty U.S. Navy landing craft rusting near a village on the shore. Patrolling the sand was difficult walking and hot. Unsurprisingly, we never found anything on the empty sands.

I employed night ambushes on the sands with the idea of catching any VC transiting them to or from our village. We never intercepted anyone coming or going. This was a populated area. People walked between villages all the time. The VC and the villagers were the same people, they wore the same types of clothing, and they conducted the same activities during the day. I wish I'd had an interpreter.

We also manned our compound's fortifications during the night. The east side was shy of suitable fortifications. The south side was defended by a South Vietnamese Regional Force/Provincial Force of about fifteen poorly trained and, near as I could tell, worthless militia and no fortifications.

It was easy duty if we stayed out of the deserted and booby-trapped area at the north end of our village and no one attacked us.

The villagers had access to my medic for those illnesses and injuries from which we all suffer from time to time. In essence, we operated a permanent mini–MEDCAP. We did not abuse them in any way. There would be no "Ugly American" incidents.

There Really Are Stupid Questions

On the second day of my return to 1st Platoon, I decided to test fire and adjust the telescopic sight I brought back with me. The top of the sand dune overlooking the deserted area seemed the perfect place to shoot. I "borrowed" one of my squads, one of my machine gunners (Frenchie, who came from New Jersey not France) and took them and the new lieutenant with me. I brought the squad for protection while we shot from exposed positions. Frenchie needed to test fire his M-60 machine gun to work off the burr on its new bolt.

The lieutenant came along because technically I did not yet command the 1st Platoon. I did not intend to usurp his command in any way. I "suggested" this expedition rather than giving orders. It was another beautiful day, clear with a comfortable temperature.

When we reached the top of the slope, I sat cross-legged in a classic shooter's seated position with my left side sort of pointing into the booby-trapped area. Frenchie was standing about five feet in front of me. We fired in the same direction. The squad and the new lieutenant lay on the sand about ten meters behind us, safely out of the line of any incoming fire from the booby-trapped area. Some Viet Cong remained in the area and I did not want to unnecessarily place the new lieutenant or the men at risk.

Shooting for accuracy dictated I fire single rounds at a target in the booby-trapped area and adjust the sight accordingly. Frenchie fired single rounds to work the burr off his M-60's bolt. We made adjustments to our weapons after each of our shots, he to his M-60 and me to my M-16's scope.

The distinctive sound of an AK-47 firing a long burst on fully automatic shattered the calm of the morning. It was close to us. At the same time, I saw spouts of sand directly in front of us jumping from the impact of those bullets from the AK-47. It was exactly like you see in the movies, except these were real.

I instantly switched to fully automatic, aimed at where I thought the AK-47 had fired and pulled the trigger. I had eighteen empty casings glistening in an arc in less than two seconds.

Out of the corner of my eye, I saw Frenchie firing at a more distant bunch of bushes. He was working his way through a hundred-round belt of ammunition. I saw the metal links from the belt piling up around his ankles.

The scene was one of loud noises from weapons firing fully automatic with wisps of gun smoke from our weapons and the oil smoking off my rifle's s barrel, and many ejected casings glittering in the sun.

I was making a rapid change of magazines when the new lieutenant came running up to me. I give him high marks for bravery for that. Frenchie still fired his machine gun. As God is my witness, the new lieutenant shouted, "WHAT ARE YOU DOING?" For a split second, I was speechless.

Teachers tell us there is no such thing as a stupid question. Here, only a second ago, I had been asked one in the midst of a potential firefight! I looked directly at him while answering calmly, "I'm shootin'." I inserted the full magazine into my M-16, chambered a round and started to pull the trigger.

This new lieutenant clearly misinterpreted our rules of engagement. He persevered by telling me returning fire was not allowed until I took casualties. I will give him high marks for perseverance too.

I experienced another microsecond of incredulity before I told him I'd reopened a cut from shaving that morning. That settled, I pulled the trigger to empty my second magazine in the hope of hitting the VC who fired his AK-47 at Frenchie and me.

Immediately after firing the second magazine, I called to the squad to send up the M-72 anti-tank rocket they brought with them. When I got it, I fired it into the booby-trapped area. I received some training on them in OCS but never fired one, which explains how I completely missed the large, booby-trapped area and hit the bay.

Later I explained two things to the new lieutenant. The first is the rules of engagement permit us to defend ourselves. Frenchie and I did that. The second was I always take it personal when people shoot at me. Good thing he got the job as the XO. It gave him time to learn about some of the commonsense aspects of combat. Fortunately, we had no casualties.

The Viet Cong who fired at us is a very brave man. I hold no animosity for him and hope he survived the war. Damn, but it was good to be home again.

Why Do We Have a Browning M-2 .50 Caliber Heavy Machine Gun?

Infantry companies are not equipped for the M-2. Nor are infantrymen trained on it. I was told it was recently brought out to the 1st Platoon one day and dropped off without the tools to adjust it for firing or any cleaning equipment for it. This happened before I returned from Rio. It was dirty and rusted. From whence or why this one came, I never knew.

The M-2 needs a simple adjustment to ensure that the bolt does not strike the end of the barrel when firing. Neither the tool to do this nor the tool to adjust the timing mechanism to enable the gun to fire in the fully automatic mode came with it. Without a properly adjusted firing mechanism, the gun could not fire.

As luck would have it, I had completed the Advanced Individual Training (AIT) course for a tank crewman prior to going to OCS. My training included the M-2 with an emphasis on rapidly taking it apart and reassembling it in firing condition. I was the fastest in my class. I succeeded in cleaning this one with the cleaning equipment that came with my M-16, which required a lot of elbow grease and improvisation.

Armor School instructors at Ft. Knox taught my classmates and me two field expedient methods to make an M-2 battle ready if you lacked the special tools that came with it. I reached far back into my memory to pull up those methods. The first method worked like a charm. I screwed the barrel in all the way and unscrewed it three clicks. Now the bolt could not strike the end of the barrel during firing. The second method set the timing so the gun could fire semi and fully automatic. My training worked beautifully. The M-2 did too. We used it at night to fire into the booby-trapped area to disrupt anything the Viet Cong might be planning or simply to terrify them. The deep sound of a .50 caliber projectile passing close overhead does this exceptionally well.

It is still in use on our armored vehicles. It is, and remains, my favorite weapon even if it is too heavy to be physically carried into battle. It fires a projectile about the length and width of the two end segments of a man's forefinger. Its sound dominates the sound of small arms on the battlefield. I used to refer to it as the "E.F. Hutton" of the battlefield because everybody stops to listen when it speaks. Its deep sound is truly impressive.

Stupid Questions Are More Common Than I Thought

The company command post and the 1st Platoon came under sniper fire one night a week or so after the first incident. Some dedicated soul, probably the same one, kept firing his AK-47 at us. I saw burst after burst of tracers from an AK-47 fire streaking over us. The tracers looked like they came from the inland edge of the "beach" where more villagers lived. The edge was around twenty meters directly east of us.

I strode across our compound to retrieve my M-16. I deliberately "strode" so my men saw me moving with a purpose and self-confidence like this sort of thing is an everyday occurrence. It helps to keep them from taking an unwise and precipitate action.

I passed the mortar crew leader lying flat on the ground. I told him I wanted an illumination round over the edge of the sand dune and pointed to where I wanted it. He gave his crew the firing data without ever getting up and exposing himself to the AK-47 rounds passing above him. The mortar round was right on the money. A parachute flare burst into a bright light directly over the edge of the sand and the villagers who lived there. It put light on all the eastern approaches to our east side perimeter. I was impressed.

I got my rifle and headed out to the Browning M-2. Fortunately, the M-2 was emplaced on the east side of the compound and protected by sandbags. I sat down at the gunner's position and prepared to fire it. Overkill against an AK-47? Perhaps, but let's not forget I take it exceedingly personal when someone shoots at me.

It takes two pulls with the charging handle on an M-2 to chamber a round before it may be fired. I was on the second pull of the M-2's charging handle when my CO walked up to me. He asked, "What are you doing?" I thought it looked obvious, what with me sitting behind the gun, pulling the charging handle to put a round in the chamber, and one thumb near the trigger. I answered him respectfully, "I'm fixin' to shoot." He told me "No; there are civilians in that direction." I made one attempt to change his mind by reminding him every hut in that direction had an underground bunker and surely all the villagers were down in them already.

He stood firm and he was correct to do so. But he did say I could use a 40 mm grenade launcher to fire some 40 mm grenades into the area along the east side of our perimeter but short of the huts. It was a good idea designed to discourage anyone trying to sneak up to the perimeter in the dark. I fired about twelve "grenades" into that area. The check of the area in daylight disclosed no bodies or the blood trails of wounded VC.

Life in pacification tends to be boring and repetitive. These factors often lead to a combat unit losing its edge. Perhaps the reason why the 3rd Battalion replaced the 1st Battalion had to do with the 1st getting its edge back. I worried about this happening to us. A sufficient number of things happened in the weeks leading up to my promotion to keep life interesting.

My comment about not having a career in the Army came back to haunt me. My CO prepared my Officer Evaluation Report (OER) shortly before I promoted to captain and before he transferred back to the United States. He checked the box "Do Not Promote Ahead of Contemporaries" because I told him I had no interest in going career.

The captain running S-1 brought this to my attention after my former company commander went home. It was a career killer. At his urging, I submitted a letter with the OER explaining how my former company commander came to check that box and neither of us knew it automatically made the otherwise glowing OER a negative one. My letter worked because years later I was promoted to major in the Army Reserves. Months later, and before I left active duty, I decided to go career with the Reserves.

17

A Man Killed
by a Claymore Mine
and RF/PFs

The day I regained command of the 1st Platoon, one of my squads was sent to patrol the booby-trapped village. Less than fifteen minutes had elapsed since the squad left, when I heard the characteristic sound of a Claymore mine detonating. With a sinking feeling, I scanned for the dirty gray smoke which accompanied such an explosion. I saw it in the booby-trapped area of the village. It was exactly where the squad would've reached if it patrolled at a normal walking pace.

Within seconds, the squad called over the radio requesting a "Dust-off" (another name for a medevac helicopter) for the wounded paratrooper. Then the squad picked up their wounded comrade and carried him out of the booby-trapped area to a nearby place suitable for a helicopter to land.

The dust-off went off without a hitch and flew the paratrooper to the Battalion Aid Station where one of the battalion's physicians tried to save his life. About thirty minutes later, my CO received a radio notification my paratrooper had died from his wounds. He immediately told me the tragic news. A booby trap injured some of my men months earlier but this one bothered me.

I was out of the country when this young paratrooper, not long out of his training, joined the 1st Platoon. I hadn't greeted him and welcomed him to the 1st Platoon when I took command again. This informal talk usually took place over coffee or a coke. I'd tell a new man my basic expectations for him and my rules and also check to be sure he has everything necessary for combat and his personal needs.

I did not give the order which caused his death. My platoon sergeant told me these patrols originated with a standing order from my predecessor. At the time, he couldn't have known the deserted part of the village was booby-trapped with U.S. Claymore mines. I never mentioned these facts to him. He bears no fault for this young man's death.

The fault is mine. I should've asked important questions about recent orders and where the squad was going. But I didn't!

I stopped any more incursions into the booby-trapped area. I gave my sergeants strict orders to stay off the trails and paths if they entered the booby-trapped area again. I ordered no one from the 1st Platoon was to enter there without my permission and with me. If I had to send men into the booby-trapped area, I intended to lead them myself.

The next time any of my men entered the area, I led them as first in line. I lost no more paratroopers to enemy action.

18

Helping Rebuild
the Village and a Feast

September 1969

The villagers needed our help. The presence of the Viet Cong cost them more than threats and "taxation." The Viet Cong forced them to leave their ancestral home sites and live on the nearby sand where no water wells existed for drinking or hygiene and no vegetation for shade or food. They had to fetch water from the wells in the village.

The men of the 1st Platoon, except for one squad who stood guard, put down their weapons, took off their shirts and performed some pretty hard labor to help return the villagers to their ancient home sites. They did this voluntarily; I asked them, I did not order them.

I watched them carrying the large wooden roof support poles for the thatched huts, many of those poles were fifteen or more inches in diameter and up to ten or twelve feet long. It required six or more of my men to carry each of the larger poles.

My men worked day after day in sweltering temperatures and humidity until the villagers completed their move back to their ancestral home. We demonstrated conclusively that we came there to help them and not to steal from them or hurt them.

The Feast

The villagers repaid the 1st Platoon with a traditional feast. The ladies of the village outdid themselves and my men behaved like gentlemen. I sampled many new tastes. All of the food creations were exceptional, except the snails. Everybody, villager and soldier alike, enjoyed this affair. I hope they remember us with good thoughts. From this moment forward, we had a good relationship with the village. Pacification only works if the parties have this sort of relationship.

These good and proud people are no different from us in many respects. I made sure my men understood this point. They were to treat the villagers with courtesy and respect. I am not saying this because I am a do-gooder or to make myself look good. I'm thick-skinned so I rarely care what anyone thinks of me. This time was no exception. I did what was right for those people, my men and, in a remote fashion, for my country. More wisdom gleaned from *The Ugly American*.

It turned out we really liked them. I think they liked and respected us. I watched many mornings while the lady of each thatched hut cleaned up the house. She swept the packed earth floor to get rid of anything that didn't belong there and did the same to the ground around the hut. If she had flagstones, she washed them with a little water and swept them clean. Like I said, these people are proud and possessed a quiet self-respect.

We earned their respect and trust every day by not taking advantage of them. We never demanded anything of them, never forced these people to do anything. If we needed their assistance, a rarity, we asked for it and paid for it.

My CO frequently met with the village's elders. Sometimes the meeting had to do with something that needed resolving. Other times, they met merely to say hello or ask how life was treating the other.

The villagers had access to my medic for minor injuries or illnesses. We never charged them for this. Those actions had improved our relations with the local villagers in our AO and were possibly the greatest reason they greeted us warmly when we met. Besides, they were our neighbors in every sense of the word.

We could tell local sympathies for the enemy by the greeting we received from a village, particularly if their children looked distant or, worse, cold toward us, If they did, we were in hostile territory. In that case it was wise to keep your weapons close at hand.

If the people seemed friendly and the children ran up to you playing and laughing, we probably were among friends. Keeping our weapons close was wise because we never knew when enemy forces might appear. I had no problems with these villagers or any other ones.

19

Regional Force,
Local Force and a USO Visit

October 1969

When I rejoined my platoon, I saw that a platoon of South Vietnamese Regional Force/Provincial Force (RF/PF) shared our compound with us. It is an understatement to say I was less than pleased with their presence. I never saw them do anything for the village.

They wore South Vietnamese military uniforms and carried U.S. .30 caliber carbines, none of which made them an effective fighting force. The RF/PFs lacked the good training, motivation, and discipline to make them effective soldiers. I doubted they possessed the capability to defend themselves, let alone the village. Once a day they'd leave in the morning and return in the late afternoon. I lacked any evidence to prove this, but I believed the RF/PF "soldiers" acted something like petty tyrants to the nearby villages and did nothing to help the war effort.

My defensive plans always assumed the RF/PF unit would not hold steady in the event our compound came under attack. I also worried they might throw in with the Viet Cong and turn on us. I had no way to be rid of them.

The RF/PF "soldiers" frequently supplemented their rations with birds they shot around the area. I had no problem with this, though it was disconcerting when they shot birds near the village.

The problem was the projectiles from the .30 caliber carbines they carried ricocheted off the palm trees into the village and my compound. The bullets retained enough energy to inflict serious

189

wounds or kill. I tactfully explained to the RF/PF lieutenant that his men must stop shooting into the palm trees because the ricochets could injure the very villagers he and I were there to protect.

A few days later, one of the RF/PF "soldiers" shot at birds in a palm tree again. The ricochets landed in the village and one landed in my compound with a thud. This got my Irish up but not in a blind rage.

I strode across my compound toward the barbed wire gate that opened into the village. My platoon sergeant saw the look on my face. He asked what was wrong. I said, "Get me my rifle!" He did and tossed it to me.

I went into the village to look for the man doing the shooting. I did not have to go far before I saw an RF/PF "soldier" taking aim at the top of a palm tree about seventy-five feet ahead of me. He was about to shoot at a bird,

I raised my M-16 to my shoulder, took aim, and fired three rounds around his head. I fired so rapidly my men said it sounded like I fired on fully automatic. But I'd only fired on semi-automatic mode. I'm a good shot and missed him on purpose.

I went up to the RF/PF "soldier" now seated on a log and visibly shaking. I told my interpreter to ask him why he shook. He responded he thought I was trying to kill him. Through the interpreter, I told him I did not try to kill him; but if he or anyone else continued to shoot at the birds in the palm trees I would. This is the way I ended the ricochets into the village and my compound. Message received! Message understood! Unfortunately, I had strained relations with the RF/PFs from this moment forward.

The USO Comes to My Platoon

I received word to expect a helicopter bringing two showgirls and an actor from a USO tour to our compound by the village. With the word came instructions to prepare to receive it. My compound already was large enough to land a helicopter inside it, barely. Preparations completed!

I gave my sergeants a clear set of behavior and language guidelines to convey to their men. I wanted everyone shaved and presentable and demanded the men's best behavior.

The helicopter for the USO tour arrived on time. It landed with its doors open. Inside I saw an old man with a Santa Claus–like beard and big belly seemingly dozing on the passenger bench, and there were no showgirls in sight!

My first thought was they'd brought me a wino. I later learned he was a serious actor of some fame named Tom Tully. I am sorry for thinking he was a wino. Wherever he is, I hope he accepts my apology.

My second thought was how to explain the missing girls to my men.

My third was why does the door gunner have a huge smile on his face.

Then I saw one of the girls squeezed in behind him. The other girl was behind the door gunner on the opposite side of the helicopter. Those were good reasons to smile.

I know. I'm a pig. Being politically correct means lying to yourself. I do not.

One of the ladies came from Dean Martin's "Gold Diggers." The other was a centerfold from *Playboy* magazine. They were beautiful and friendly and stayed for an hour mingling with the men. My men behaved like gentlemen the entire time.

I took a lot of verbal abuse from them when I pinned a medal on the chest of the Playmate, who wore a jungle fatigue shirt for a top. Because of the heat and humidity, she wore not much under it. I didn't peek. I felt the heat from blushing on my face.

Mr. Tully was a good sport about this. He knew my men focused their attention on the ladies.

My men really did behave like gentlemen. I'd worried for nothing; the mere presence of these beautiful women stunned them into shyness. Once again, they made me very proud to be their platoon leader.

20

Waterboarding a Female
Viet Cong Member

October 1969

Sometime in October 1969, a South Vietnamese Rural Redevelopment Unit (RDU) arrived in the area of the village the 1st Platoon protected. Their public roles were improvement of the farmer's crops and giving pro-government political education to the people. I am fairly sure they had a deeper role but I never learned exactly what it might be.

Their discipline was very good under their leader Ngoc. The government of South Vietnam armed them with World War II vintage .30 caliber carbines. It's not the weapon that makes a soldier lethal; it's using his weapons effectively. The RDU men were a much more effective military force than the RF/PF men with which I was cursed to share a position.

The reason I believed the RDU concealed a secret purpose occurred one afternoon when they wrestled a female prisoner into the 1st Platoon's compound. She was a young woman in her late teens or early twenties wearing the white blouse, black pants, and the sandals of a typical villager.

I knew only a few words or phrases in Vietnamese, but I didn't need to be fluent to see they were interrogating her. Ngoc's harsh threatening voice told me he was questioning her and probably threatening dire consequences if she refused to divulge information about the VC in the area.

I have no idea of what she said in response, but the heated, contemptuous tone in her voice and her demeanor left no doubt in my mind that she told him he would get nothing from her. Perhaps she added her assessment of his base nature and even baser ancestry.

Their exchanges became more heated with Ngoc's impatient voice becoming louder, and taking on an ominous tone. The rising level and roughness of her voice made clear her pride in opposing him. I got the impression she was openly contemptuous of Ngoc and she would not divulge anything that would harm her cause.

Ngoc gave a command. Four of his men grabbed her arms and legs and tried to stretch her face up lengthwise on the wooden bench another of his men brought. Her struggles were impressive but those men succeeded in holding her spread-eagled and face up on the bench. Another of the Ngoc's men anticipated the next step in the interrogation and had prepared for it. At a command from Ngoc, he stepped forward holding a wooden bucket.

Ngoc said something to the young woman, probably Vietnamese for talk or else. Her response was the very essence of defiance. It's fortunate my Vietnamese was far too limited to allow me to understand her.

Ngoc gave another curt order. This triggered a violent response from the young woman who tried to break free and avoid what was coming. She nearly did but more RDU men helped to hold her down. I saw her face. The look on her face showed her anger and hatred of Ngoc and his men. It also displayed the fierceness of her determination to resist. She showed no fear; although I can't imagine that she was not terrified by what came next.

The man with the bucket approached her. He took a small wet towel from the bucket and handed it to a man standing at the woman's head. This man placed it across her face and twisted it tight behind her head.

At Ngoc's command, the man with the bucket began to slowly pour water from the bucket onto the towel where it lay over her nose and mouth. The cloudiness of the water and the sparse suds meant soapy water.

The tightly twisted towel prevented the young woman from closing her mouth or twisting her head. The soapy water streamed into her mouth, into her nose, into her eyes, and probably down her throat. She was powerless to stop it or get away from it.

Her earlier struggles paled into insignificance compared to how she reacted to the burning pain in her throat, nose and eyes from the soapy water and the fear that comes to us when we cannot breathe. Her struggles became extremely violent. Herculean is not too strong a description.

At one point she managed to slide off the bench and away from the soapy water. Her respite lasted only seconds. The superior weight, number and strength of the men holding her overcame her resistance. The RDU men quickly lifted her back onto the bench and one twisted the towel tight once more. The one with the bucket poured soapy water over her face and into her mouth, nose, and eyes. She still resisted violently.

All of this torture of the young woman took place in five to ten minutes. It only ended when Ngoc realized some of my men and I were watching him waterboarding her. He gave a command and they left rapidly, taking her away either to be processed through RDU channels or to continue the interrogation somewhere with more privacy.

I never once thought I would actually witness a war crime. The waterboarding I saw came as a shock to me. Never in any of my training on the Geneva Conventions did anyone explain what action to take in such situations. Morally, I should have intervened before they fled, but they were gone.

Half a century later, I still have no clear idea of the best action to have taken in that event. I wanted to intervene. All of my options came down to potentially engaging a quasi-military force of an ally with the threat of combat or actual combat to take this young woman from them. At least my watching them made Ngoc stop the torture. I am not at all proud of this moment in my career.

Most of us have had water go up our noses or inadvertently inhaled a little of it while swimming. Water entering the nasal passages burns like hell. The amount of soapy water going into her nose, mouth, and eyes made it ten or twenty times worse for her and was indisputably torture.

20. Waterboarding a Female Viet Cong Member

In the first part of the 21st century, the American government began calling similar mistreatment of "enemy combatants" a valued "enhanced interrogation technique." To be sure, there are cosmetic differences, like plain water instead of soapy water. One is done in a clinical setting, the other in a village of thatched huts. But the sense of choking and the burn of water in the nasal passages are the same.

They use the term "enemy combatants" because the Geneva Conventions are directed to "prisoners of war" only. Ironically, the United States played a central role in the development and adoption of the concepts the Geneva Conventions are meant to protect. The humane treatment of prisoners of war on both sides of a conflict is required of every signatory. The use of torture on them to gain information is prohibited. Plus, civilians must be protected.

The United States of America has championed these concepts as far back as our Civil War. It is a signatory to the Conventions it pushed for universal adoption. The United States, as a signatory, forswore the mistreatment of captured enemy soldiers.

Every signatory, first and foremost, signed to protect their own soldiers from mistreatment when captured by an enemy! I'm sure our political class lacks any education on the history that gave birth to the Geneva Conventions. Altruism and humanitarianism played their roles, but it was enlightened national self-interest which caused many nations to sign those Conventions.

Many of our elected officials, leaders of our intelligence agencies and some in our Armed Forces, with the American flag figuratively draped around their shoulders, bought into the arguments to define those captured terrorists as "enemy combatants" because they did not wear uniforms or serve any specific nation. This class calls the mistreatment of the terrorists we capture "enhanced interrogation techniques."

They pat themselves on the back for their brilliance in finding a way around the Geneva Conventions. Lawyers employ this sort of dishonesty. It has earned lawyers the disfavor of many in our society, except politicians and other lawyers.

The United States has condoned the use of torture—sorry, an "enhanced interrogation technique"—on whomever they label "enemy combatants." If memory serves me, we soundly and rightfully condemned the Nazis for using torture on the members of several resistance organizations' men and women who did not wear uniforms and were captured on and off the battlefields. Such reprehensible behavior was a part of the basis for trying the Nazi and Japanese leaders on charges of committing crimes against humanity.

What our "enlightened" Democratic and Republican politicians who came up with this idea and authorized its use do not understand is the consequences of the United States publicly defining waterboarding as not being torture. Our enemies now possess a plausible justification for some day using this torture on Americans they capture.

Thanks to them, the protections of the Geneva Conventions may no longer serve to shield the men and women in the Armed Forces of the United States from greater mistreatment and torture. You know, it is difficult to take the high moral ground about your captured soldiers being abused when you are down in the sewage with the miscreants.

Perhaps the men and women who run our government should get the same training on the Geneva Conventions and the Laws of Land Warfare that I received in my training to become a commissioned officer in the U.S. Army. But then, waterboarding them is a simpler and more lasting way to teach them it is torture not interrogation.

I learned two things from this incident. First, that young woman more than earned the title of soldier. She is the bravest soldier I have ever seen. Second, waterboarding is unquestionably torture.

I am still very proud of my country. I am not proud of my country's casual adoption of torture under the irresponsible word game of calling it "enhanced interrogation techniques."

21

The Last Time I Lead My Men into Danger

November 1969

We occasionally worked a booby-trapped area to reduce the constant threat to our position it represented. The presence of Claymore mines made it difficult to conduct ground operations safely. But no minefield is perfect. We went in there once in a while to demonstrate that we could go there whenever we pleased.

My last operation involved a squad from my platoon and one from the 2nd Platoon working through the booby-trapped area from two directions. I was to come in from the east, near where a VC shot at Frenchie and me earlier. The 2nd Platoon was to come in from the southwest or opposite side. We would exit down a small ravine on the northwest side of the booby-trapped area.

I entered the booby-trapped area at the head of my squad as I said I would do. Low rows of cacti divided original home sites there. The rows of cacti remained but the thatched huts were gone. Since all of the prior booby traps were associated with the old trails through the area, I led my men away from the trails and through the cactus. I emphasized staying off the trails to them.

I learned this lesson from a combat veteran in my OCS class. A few of my men got stuck by cactus thorns. They survived. This would not have been the case if they walked on a trail and triggered a Claymore.

We reached the exit point, a short ravine leading down to the inland bay, without any more serious injuries than a cactus thorn inflicts. The ravine was steep and filled with branches from the bushes. Despite the steep incline and the somewhat tangled vegetation in the ravine, we successfully made it down to the shore of the inland bay.

Once we reached the bay, we turned to follow the shore to the right, or east. The daylight had faded but enough remained to see ducks paddling near to the shore. I snapped a shot at one of them and hit it. The men exclaimed I must be some kind of a sharp shooter. I actually missed the duck. The bullet struck the water a few feet in front of the duck and fragmented. It was one of those fragments that killed the duck. I gave the duck to the squad for a change in their diet.

I heard that characteristic explosion behind us. One of the 2nd Platoon's men triggered a Claymore. Fortunately, he survived but I never learned how badly he was wounded. They were so close to getting out of the danger area. Sometimes life stinks.

I made my usual rounds of the men later that night. Everything was in order. I expected my sergeants to have everything correct but I checked because checking was part of my leadership responsibilities. These veterans were very experienced. I like to think they appreciated I checked up on them from time to time. They knew I wanted to make sure things were as they should be in order to save their lives. They also knew I was not looking for a petty reason to discipline them.

I walked up to my new fan club while they ate dinner. They offered me a taste of the duck, which I accepted graciously as befits a sharpshooter. They'd prepared it as a sort of duck stew. The duck was tough but tasty. More important, my men's spirits were high. My replacement would be most fortunate to command these men. I knew I was fortunate practically from the beginning.

My birthday came not long before my promotion to captain and reassignment to a staff position. I received nothing from home on my birthday. A week before I was promoted, I received a birthday card from my mother. It was postmarked ten days after my birthday.

She wrote she had forgotten my birthday. I wondered how she forgot it; she was there. She also informed me my little sister had made tollhouse cookies for me. She related how the cookies had come out perfect and tasted great. So good my family had eaten them. They ate my birthday cookies? How is this possible? Why tell me?

On the nineteenth of November I was promoted to the rank of captain.

22

A Captain on the Battalion's Operations Staff

19 November 1969 to 9 March 1970

Assistant Operations Officer

My promotion to the rank of captain came with a transfer to the battalion's Headquarters Company. I bid goodbye to my men, keeping it brief to avoid making a fool of myself. Then I left on the helicopter sent to get me.

I already knew I'd been assigned to the battalion's S-3, the Operations Staff Section. The battalion commander issued advice or orders to the S-3's Battalion's Operations Officer, Major Donald Soland, later Brigadier General Soland. He put together plans for combat operations and monitored the operations as they progressed. No plan was ready without his final approval. The S-3 recommends changes to the battalion commander after the plans were set in motion or the situation on the ground changed.

I was the First Officer Assistant to Major Soland. I enjoyed serving under him and learned much of what I know about the role of an assistant operations officer from him. I didn't know it at the time but what I would learn as an assistant operations and training staff officer from him opened another military career window for me.

He was what we called a Five Per Center. This meant the Army Promotion Boards rated him in the top five percent of those of his rank being considered for promotion and made him eligible for early promotion. Later, I learned he continued to be promoted early. I ran across him in Germany during a large-scale staff exercise in the early eighties. He wore the star of a brigadier general, more proof the Army gets it right sometimes. He passed away a long time ago.

I ran the day-to-day aspects of the Main Tactical Operation Center (TOC) on the battalion's rear area at LZ Uplift. I didn't make recommendations on how to fight the war in our area since that was for those above me. Part of my job was knowing where the rifle companies were and what they were doing. I had to be able to provide this information virtually instantly when asked.

If I couldn't make contact with Maj. Soland, I might be asked to provide information to the battalion commander about some part of the operation taking place. This never happened. Fortunately, it rarely does.

The job does sound rather boring, doesn't it? It wasn't. I worked twelve or more hours of every day, seven days a week, no weekends or holidays off, no overtime pay, no comp time and was on call every night in the event a problem came up. I had to make sure everything that happened, including radio traffic and telephone calls, were recorded in detail in our daily historical log.

Occasionally something came up but nothing major. Meaning, no getting drunk for me. For instance, one night a soldier on guard duty thought he saw something, which he interpreted as an enemy sneaking toward him. He fired several shots from his M-16. The duty officer sent for me. When I arrived, I heard more shots from the guard. There was no return gun fire from an enemy. We were not under attack.

Before I could do or say anything, I saw one of the S-3's RTOs moving toward and reaching for the big red button that triggers the sirens, which gets everybody up to defend LZ Uplift.

It was like watching two trains about to collide in slow motion and being unable to shout a warning to prevent it. He hit the button before I could stop him. The trains collided. At that point, I waited for various officers to arrive. We turned off the sirens. I told the RTOs to begin calling every unit to let them know it was a false alarm.

The air officer arrived half-dressed and barefoot with his M-16 in one hand and his sandals in the other, the high point for me. The low point? Documenting this in the daily historical log. I took no action against the RTO beyond letting him know that only Maj. Soland or I could authorize sounding the alarm.

This same RTO also decided to tell one of the company commanders it was okay to move his company's AO. I think the major explained to him that only the battalion commander or he had that authority. Otherwise, he performed well as an RTO.

Maj. Soland spent most days with the battalion commander. They used the command-and-control helicopter to travel back and forth to the Forward Command Post or to look over the progress of the battalion's rifle companies from the air.

They alternated remaining overnight at the Forward Command Post, which lacked many of the amenities of LZ Uplift. Chief among those missing amenities was a shower. Maj. Soland often radioed us with a "Flaming Arrow" message late in the afternoon. If the NVA were listening, I hoped trying to figure what new combat plans and orders we had created gave them fits.

A "Flaming Arrow" message simply meant for us to light the immersion heaters in the officer's shower to provide hot water for the major or the battalion commander to use when they got back to LZ Uplift.

When the major came back, we used the information he brought back to update the Viet Cong's trails and fortifications on the battalion's master map. The units on the ground supplied most of this information. This map showed the latest locations of friendly units and enemy units on it too. I transferred the latest friendly unit information to the map in the TOC's briefing room every day before the evening briefing. The S-2 intelligence officer bore the responsibility for placing the information on enemy units on the map.

For the first event of most mornings, we briefed the pilots of the helicopter assigned to us as the command-and-control helicopter for the day. First, we always had coffee ready for them to help counter any effects of any festivities of the previous evening at their bases. Our air officer gave the briefing. I assisted as necessary, primarily with unit locations and their missions.

An important task, perhaps a critical task, for our air officer, was plugging a Y-cord into the command-and-control helicopter's internal wiring for the crew's helmets and the radios. This allowed the major to communicate over the helicopter's intercom system or its more powerful radios. An ordinary PRC–25 radio, the same type my platoon's RTOs carried, was installed for the battalion commander's use. It was not as flexible or as powerful as the helicopter's radio system.

Our battalion commander was not the sharpest knife in the drawer. The major did not want him to give unwise orders to the companies until they discussed the situation. I suspect he was another lieutenant colonel who came to Vietnam to get his record to show he commanded an Infantry battalion during the war. We called it "Getting his ticket punched."

One thing I must include in any discussion of the S-3. Occasionally I had a lot of time on my hands. We created a fictional corporation called Soland Air Lines, abbreviated SAL. Its aircraft were the helicopters that flew for us. We even issued stock certificates. The logo was a standing white duck with a large peace symbol emblazoned on its chest and a long scarf in Infantry's light blue color tied to its left leg. The major and the pilots thought it was funny. We gave the pilots stock certificates in SAL.

The radio traffic on the battalion's radios was rarely overwhelming in amount but I needed to be kept apprised of its content. If the major gave instructions to do something, I damn well better have known about it and got it done. If I did not hear the radio traffic, the RTOs had orders to let me know immediately. In the event of an emergency or a time critical action the order was to send someone to get me if I was out of the TOC. I could be at the mess hall for a meal or in my quarters after hours.

I briefed the duty officer each night on his responsibilities and the basic emergency procedures, which meant getting me. Anything beyond that required sending for Maj. Soland or contacting him by radio.

I didn't always eat lunch or dinner in the mess hall because of the press of my duties. In these instances, the steak house became a lifesaver. I would ask one of the RTOs to take a long lunch or sometimes dinner break, give him five dollars and ask him to buy a steak, beans and a coke for me at the steak house on the way back. I don't know how the steak house was able to get steaks when the mess hall could not, but the steaks and beans were excellent.

Another USO Tour

One rather interesting event marked my early days in the S-3. Another USO Tour stopped at LZ Uplift. I don't remember much about it because learning the position and taking care of my duties kept me too busy in the TOC. I did go out for a few minutes to see who was in this USO Tour. I recognized her as Ina Balin. She was a famous actress of considerable note and beautiful beyond mere words.

I am certain Ms. Balin possessed a great heart because she went out of her way to speak with the men and did it in a friendly and honest manner. She had a smile for everyone. I only watched her interacting with the men for a few minutes before my duties took me back into the TOC. She left an indelible mark. I remembered her from the 1961 movie *The Comancheros* with John Wayne and Stuart Whitman. She passed away two decades after I saw her.

Training for the Rifle Companies

We tried to rotate each company to the rear for a few days each month to give them a break from the stress of searching for the enemy. It also gave them an opportunity to rest, clean their weapons and other equipment, to get haircuts, shower and put on clean jungle fatigues and favorite of all, the chance to eat hot food in the mess hall.

It occurred to me to arrange for training for them in several basic areas. Major Soland agreed with it and gave me the go ahead.

I started with arranging with the crew chief of a medevac helicopter to teach the safe use of the "Hoist Penetrator" to the men of the rifle company temporarily back on LZ Uplift. The medevacs use this device to lift a man to the helicopter from a location where the helicopter could not land.

The Crew Chief covered the important facts. The spinning blades of a helicopter build up a tremendous charge of static electricity. If the soldiers on the ground don't allow the penetrator to touch the ground to dissipate the electricity, the charge is enough to knock a man down or into unconsciousness, thus creating an additional casualty. The first demonstration showed how to safely ground the penetrator and dissipate the electric charge.

The second demonstration focused on securely strapping the injured person to the penetrator. This is critical. If not done properly, the man could slip from it. Depending on the height above ground or his injuries, the man could receive additional injuries or die.

Each demonstration used a medevac helicopter either sitting on the ground or hovering about fifty feet above the ground. I learned things I didn't know from this segment.

Next came training for the RTOs from the technicians from the Signal Office. The topic was how to take care of their radios. Many of the radio operators had never received formal training on the PRC-25s they carried and used beyond changing the batteries and changing frequencies. The technicians discussed and demonstrated the basic preventive maintenance that can be done by soldiers in the field.

I learned some new information from this training. The PRC-25 radios have what appear to be two handles on the radio's face. I always thought they were handles and used them as such. They are not handles; they're not strong enough. They are there to protect the face of the radio from impacts by large objects when mounted horizontally in vehicles or placed on desks or shelves like the larger radios in the TOC.

The last topic of instruction gave refresher training to the medics on giving plasma transfusions in the field. Plasma, derived from human blood with the red blood cells and the clotting factors filtered out, does not require constant refrigeration as blood does, so medics can carry it in the field.

Plasma is a blood expander transfused into a soldier in danger of bleeding out. It helps maintain the proper volume of liquid in his circulatory system which it needs to keep it from collapsing, and to keep him alive until he reaches a battalion field hospital where blood transfusions are available.

Although the medics hadn't received this refresher training for some time, they could be called upon to give plasma transfusions in the field at any moment. If I were to be the recipient of such a transfusion, I wanted to know the medic was current on inserting the needle into a vein.

My nights usually revolved around dinner, followed by Pinochle games in the officers' quarters and early to bed. I finally learned to play the game well. We played in the common room where the music and the bar could be found.

Gunships for the Tet Holiday of 7 February 1970

Somebody high up in the chain of command received intelligence saying another enemy offensive might happen on Tet of 1970. As a result, we were placed on a heightened alert status. The Army dispersed its air assets. We received two UH-1 helicopter gunships from the 5th Special Forces Group's helicopter company in Nha Trang for a couple weeks, call sign Wolf Pack.

I knew their arrival had the potential to be interesting when I saw a large (three feet by four feet by two feet) thermal box, intended for the cold transportation of blood for transfusions, in one helicopter. To these helicopter crews, it had become a large and well-made picnic cooler partially filled with beer and ice. When I asked why they brought it, one pilot said they couldn't find out if we had beer available. They felt better after I told them about the steak house where they could purchase beer and a good steak.

They had nothing to do for those two weeks. I received no instructions regarding what I was to do with them. More importantly, I received no instructions telling me what I couldn't do with them! I did not ask for clarifying instructions because that would interfere with a couple of plans beginning to bubble to the surface of my mind. I interpreted the lack of prohibitive instructions to mean they were mine to control for the period if they were willing and I proposed nothing outrageous.

Emergency situations were different. If the Army needed these gunships somewhere, we were given the information to pass to the pilots. I gave them the type of mission, the radio frequency, call sign, map location and a synopsis of the ground situation of the unit they were to support.

Later, this situation came up for us. A UH-1 helicopter without mini-guns and rockets reported seeing a handful of enemy soldiers, NVA or VC, under some trees in a valley on the far side of the hill on the north side of LZ Uplift. I gave the information to the gunships and asked them to check out the situation. They scrambled within five minutes and headed north over that hill.

Later the pilots told me that as soon as they crested the hill and started to descend, they saw the enemy directly ahead of them practically in their sights. They fired several rockets at them with devastating effect. A ground force sent later to assess the damage found nothing identifiable but a boot. The NVA wore boots, the Viet Cong didn't.

On another day, the gunships were tasked to escort a medevac helicopter to pick up a wounded soldier from one of the other battalions. I flew along as an observer. The pick-up had to be made via a hoist penetrator through a large opening or hole down through the thick triple canopy jungle to the jungle floor. A problem arose when the lack of wind at ground level left the ground unit's marking smoke trapped under the trees adjacent to the hole. The medevac pilot could not see the smoke to identify the pick-up point.

The pilot of the gunship I was in flew his aircraft into the hole to mark the pick-up for the medevac. The hole was big enough for the gunship to fly along its walls at five knots airspeed (about six mph). However, the gunship was not designed for this kind of flying environment and threatened to stall and crash into the jungle.

The pilot used as much power as he could get from the

helicopter's engine to keep his aircraft in the air. The helicopter shuddered and shook noticeably, but didn't crash.

The medevac pilot radioed he saw the gunship flying in the hole. We got out of the hole. The medevac descended to the hole and retrieved the wounded soldier. The Army possessed some of the best helicopter pilots in the world in Vietnam. The two flying that gunship must be among the very best or the most insane.

One day, one of the pilots, while flying back from a mission, reported seeing something suspicious on a hill not far from our perimeter. I had no one to send to investigate even if I could get permission.

I donned my load bearing harness and asked him to fly me out to take a look. When we arrived, I saw what looked like a stack of dried palm fronds. I could not think of a reason why they should be there a half-mile from the village just outside our perimeter. The pilot hovered low over the hillside to let me off to investigate on the ground. I told the pilot I wanted to go alone but he sent one of his door gunners with me as a precaution. I found this out when I heard one of the door gunners alight behind me.

The gunner and I made our way through some moderately thick brush and low trees until we reached the palm fronds. I saw nothing about them or the surrounding area that indicated any kind of threat to LZ Uplift. To be certain, I set fire to them. They went up in flames, along with about half of the hillside.

I started using the gunships for last light checks around LZ Uplift's perimeter. They flew around the perimeter, with me as an observer, looking for signs of an imminent attack. It didn't hurt that these gunships look different from UH-1 transports. Our gunships had a well-deserved reputation for killing the NVA and VC.

We didn't see anything. We weren't attacked while the gunships stayed with us. We hadn't been attacked prior to their arrival or after their departure either. Since part of my job was to protect LZ Uplift, I saw no harm in this activity.

The obvious presence of the gunships would require the enemy to rethink any plans to attack LZ Uplift. It does pay to advertise. At the conclusion of one of these flights the battalion's XO saw me jump from the gunship after it landed, wearing the extra armor the door gunners wore. He grounded me.

The Tet threat never materialized. The gunships flew home, with more beer in the thermo box. Nothing lasts forever.

An Alcoholic Battalion Commander

An especially disquieting event took place in the TOC while I worked late one night. The enlisted men in the TOC and I were working on copying some documents in the back room. In the pre–Xerox era, they used a wet process machine. It's a bit tedious and messy but all we had for this important work. We had to complete the copying.

Maj. Soland was in the room with us but further to the back studying our master trail map. Then the battalion commander entered.

He was unquestionably drunk. He lit into me about the length of my hair. In the field, I had no means to get it cut; consequently, I never gave it much thought. I'd forgotten to get it cut. He chewed me out, cursed me, and left.

Maj. Soland came over to me, visibly angry, not at me, but at the battalion commander. He apologized for what happened. The battalion commander had chewed me out in front of the enlisted men who were my subordinates. This is a gross violation of protocol. It could negatively affect their respect for me. It didn't.

I thanked Maj. Soland for his concern but reminded him I did not plan on being a career soldier and sergeants had chewed me out in my enlisted days. I lack any evidence, but I am fairly sure Maj. Soland spoke privately with the battalion commander about this. I got my hair cut the next day. I had allowed it to grow too long.

23

Time to Go Home

During January and early February of 1970, I thought a lot about another six-month extension of my tour in Vietnam. I had enough time left in my active service obligation to do it. The time to submit the paperwork before I was sent back to the United States drew closer. One morning I woke up, I don't remember the date, and thought to myself, "I'm tired. I think I'll go home." I didn't submit the papers. I was sent home on March 9, 1970, twenty-five months after I arrived in Vietnam.

24

Awards and Decorations

For my Vietnam service, I received a Combat Infantryman Badge, two Bronze Star Medals, an Air Medal, an Army Commendation Medal, a Vietnam Service Medal with one silver and one bronze campaign star and a Bronze campaign star for participation in seven campaigns.

The 3rd Brigade, 82nd Airborne Division received a Valorous Unit Award, which I'm entitled to wear.

I also received the following foreign decorations: The Republic of Vietnam Campaign medal with 1960 Device.

The 3rd Brigade, 82nd Airborne Division received the Vietnamese Cross of Gallantry Medal unit award with Palm and the Vietnamese Civil Action Medal unit award with Palm while I served with it, both of which I'm entitled to wear.

The 173rd Airborne Brigade received the Vietnamese Cross of Gallantry Medal unit award with Palm and the Vietnamese Civil Action Medal unit award with Palm while I served with it, which I'm entitled to wear. However, the U.S. Army Regulations do not permit wearing second or subsequent awards of either of them.

Epilogue

Years later, I learned why we could not locate any Viet Cong or NVA to engage. President Johnson had turned the U.S. Air Force and U.S. Navy pilots loose on the enemy. We originally thought the NVA suffered 40,000 fatalities in their Tet Offensive of 1968. After the war ended the North said it was 50,000. There was practically no one with whom to do battle for the next two years. The VC were virtually eliminated.

My men trusted me to do my job well, all day every day. All of us hoped I wouldn't make mistakes that could get them wounded or killed. The obligations which flowed from this trust stayed in the forefront of my thinking every day.

My obligations to them and their trust in me are two sides of the coin of loyalty. Loyalty must flow in both directions at every level of an organization, public or private, if it is to be successful. Commanders who forget their duty of loyalty to the men and women they command are rarely considered great. All too often, loyalty exists in name only.

I accomplished each of my missions. I didn't succeed in keeping all my men alive or in one piece. Some call it the fortunes of war. They are correct to a point. I know casualties are a part of war; I also know I carry little blame for their injuries or their deaths. However, I hold to the view that no such thing as acceptable losses exists!

I knew my men, their names, their faces, their voices and some things about their personal lives. Many nights we tried to ignore the buzzing of hordes of mosquitoes, or the rain and the mud, or the heat and the humidity, in the hope of getting a few hours of sleep. I remember some faces when I tell anecdotes about those days. Unfortunately, with the passing of each year, their names, their faces and the anecdotes become more shrouded in the mists of time, hence this memoir.

I returned from Vietnam self-confident, in good health, and much older than my years. Leading my paratroopers permanently changed me from the somewhat naïve young man who arrived in the dark pre-dawn hours of Chu Lai in early 1968.

I am mentally fine beyond a pronounced dislike for politicians who choose to ignore their oaths to "support and defend the Constitution of the United States against all enemies, foreign and domestic; that I will bear true faith and allegiance to the same; that I take this obligation freely, without any mental reservation or purpose of evasion; and that I will well and faithfully discharge the duties of the office on which I am about to enter," especially the parts about they "will bear true faith and allegiance to the same" and "will well and faithfully discharge the duties of the office I am about to enter." My men fulfilled the same oath! Why can't they?

I think this last point encompasses most politicians in the federal government.

Oddly enough, my time in Vietnam turned out to be one of the best in my life. My job happened to be important, a job at which I became rather proficient. I helped make a small part of history.

American paratroopers, I'm not talking about me, have demonstrated every time they parachute from an aircraft in flight, and in more than one war, that they possess the same courage, honor and loyalty as any of the finest soldiers in the great armies of history. The men I led served their time in Vietnam with the same courage, honor, loyalty, a rough grace, and maybe with a little resignation at times. Amazingly, they shouldered their heavy rucksacks, took up their weapons, and endured the vicissitudes of weather and terrain with a modicum of good humor every day.

Their morale may have ebbed from time to time but it never broke. Soldiers never faltered in our seemingly endless marches to find the enemy. They were always battle ready and meant to prevail.

I consider them to be heroes. Not because of those rare moments of extraordinary courage in the face of danger, but in the marching to possible battles day after day, loaded down like pack mules, in harsh unforgiving terrain, in the heat and humidity of summer, or the cold and near constant rains of the monsoon season, never knowing when a bullet or booby trap might find them.

My paratroopers, like the Spartans, willingly obeyed the laws of their nation and the orders of their superiors despite knowing their obedience to those laws and orders could mean terrible injury or certain death for them. They would have met whatever we faced with courage and a fierce determination to win. I don't have the words to tell you how very proud I am of the men I led.

I retired as a United States Army Parachutist and Special Forces qualified Infantry Major, with specialties of Operations and Training Staff Officer and Psychological Operations Staff Officer. I'm very proud of that and my service.

Looking back, the years of my military service leading an airborne rifle platoon in combat operations is far and above the best job I've ever had. In the words of Lou Gehrig in his 1939 closing speech to the fans, "...I consider myself the luckiest man on the face of this earth."

Index

Numbers in **bold italics** indicate pages with illustrations

Index

Index

for wounded Paratrooper 126; ice cream 39–40, 93, 95–97; LZ Uplift steak house 175, 204; pooling C-rations on mountain top 162; resupply day 164; village feast 186–187

Fort Benning, Georgia 20

Fort Bragg, North Carolina 3–8, 23–24, 56, 138

Fort Knox, Kentucky 180

Forward Air Controller (FAC) 27–29

Forward Observer (FO) 64–65

fragmentation grenades 14–15, 62, 109

Frenchie (machine gunner) 178–179

FTD florist shop 169

Gallantry Cross Unit Citation with Palm 31, 211

Gehrig, Lou 214

Geneva Conventions 194–196

Gia Le Combat Base: Dorn as Public Information Officer (PIO) 19–21, 27–32; mail 18–19; military strength 15; NVA attack on 22–23, 50, 52; staff life 17–20; surprise reunion 20–21; 3rd Brigade Headquarters 17, *18*

graves, Vietnamese 88, 152

grenades: fragmentation grenades 14–15, 62, 109; smoke grenades 14, 62, 79, 96, 106, 154; white phosphorus grenades 109

H&I (harassing and interdiction) fires 159–160

Hai Van Pass, Vietnam 15, 36, 38–40

ham radio 47

Hamburger Hill 29

hammock 148

harassing and interdiction (H&I) fires 159–160

Hawaii, Dorn's R&R 174

Headquarters Company, 1st Battalion, 508th PIR 50–55

helicopters: AH-1 Cobra helicopter gunship 23; along river south of Saigon *90*; 1st Platoon, C Company, 3rd Battalion, 503rd PIR pickup 153–155; medevac operations 125, 184, 204–205, 207–208; medical rescue flight 133–134; passenger capacity 154; pilot skills 207–208; pineapple plantation reconnaissance mission 81–83; Reconnaissance Platoon, E Company extraction 125; resupply *73*; rooftop landing sites 59–60; Tet holiday (1970) 206–208

Hill 15 102–103, 104, 106

Ho Chi Minh Trail 28, 53

Hope, Bob 101, 107

hot dog, for wounded Paratrooper 126

Hué, Vietnam 15, 16, 40, 45–46

human skull, carried by Paratrooper 152

humidity 6–7, 12, 32

hygiene 33–34

ice cream 39–40, 93, 95–97

illnesses, Dorn's 43–44, 74–75

"JJ" (radio telephone operator) 66–68

Johnson, Lyndon 6, 14, 212

Killy, Jean-Claude 79

Kit Carson Scout 84–86, *85*

Korean War 8

"land navigation" skills 64–66, 90–91

Landing Zone *see* LZ

Laws of Land Warfare 196

leave *see* special leave

leeches 158

"Legs" (not airborne qualified) 64

liberation of items: by Dorn at PX Depot in Da Nang 37–38, 46; by Dorn, of armchair from Officer's Club 44–45; by 2nd Battalion, 505th PIR in Da Nang 15–16

Long Binh, Vietnam 101, 107, 109–110

loyalty 70, 212

LZ (Landing Zone) English 118, 133–134

LZ (Landing Zone), 1st Platoon, C Company, 3rd Battalion, 503rd PIR 155–156, 175–178

LZ (Landing Zone) Uplift: Dorn's trip to 118–119; 1st Battalion, 503rd PIR 118–119, 122–123, 127–128, 175; NVA and VC soldiers 207; perimeter checks 208; reconnaissance of nearby village 127–128; Reconnaissance Platoon, E Company 122–123, 127; steak house 175, 204; 3rd Battalion, 503rd PIR 175–178, 201–202; USO Tours 190–191, 204

M-72 anti-tank rocket 179

M-16A1 rifle 8, 114–115, 118, 178–179, 181, 190

M-60 machine gun 178–179

M-2 .50 caliber heavy machine gun 180–181, 182

mail 18–19

mangrove swamps 90, 91

maps: "land navigation" skills 64–66, 90–91; mudflats 90–91; 1:50,000 scale topographic maps 89–90; 1:25,000 scale Picto-Supplement maps 89–90; 3rd Battalion, 503rd PIR master map 202

Marines *see* U.S. Marine Corps

MARS (Military Affiliated Radio Station) 47

Martin, Dean 191

218

Index

meals *see* food

medevac helicopters 125, 184, 204–205, 207–208

Medical Civic Action Programs (MEDCAPS) 21–22, 102–104

Miami, Florida 170–171

Military Affiliated Radio Station (MARS) 47

Military Police (MPs) 15, 32

mines 87; *see also* "Bouncing Betty" mines; Claymore mines

Moltke, Karl Graf von 69

monsoons 7, 32

morale: battle-ready 213; Dorn's leadership 95, 151–152, 198; food and 73, 198; lack of information and 151–152; mail and 18–19; miscarriage of justice 132; wounded soldiers 125–126

mortars 146, 157, 181

motor pool 32

MPs (Military Police) 15, 32

mudflats: crossing 92–93; dangers 92; drowned Paratrooper 97–98; search and destroy operation 89–95, 97–98; Viet Cong fortifications 94–95

napalm 14, 51

Napoleon 156

National Route 1A, Vietnam 35–36, 38; *see also* Hai Van Pass

National Route QL-1, Vietnam 118, 131

Navy *see* U.S. Navy

near death experiences: acute interstitial pneumonia 75; blood poisoning 74–75; Da Nang rocket attack 41–43; dizziness and unconsciousness en route to Da Nang 43–44; Dorn as bulletproof 78

Ngoc (RDU leader) 192–194

Nha Trang 206

97th Company 20

Nipa palms 90, 91, 92–93

Noncommissioned Officer Candidate School 67

Normandy *see* D-Day

North Vietnamese Army (NVA): A Shau Valley 28–29; attack on Gia Le Combat Base 22–23, 50, 52; capture by Air Force pilot 27; Da Nang rocket attack 41–43; Ho Chi Minh Trail 28; LZ Uplift area fortifications 122–125; regiment decimated by 3rd Brigade 30–32; Tet holiday (1970) 207; Tet Offensive 6, 13, 20, 54, 123, 212

Nypa palms *see* Nipa palms

Officer Candidate School (OCS) 65, 67, 77, 115, 197

Officer Evaluation Report (OER) 182–183

Omaha Beach, Normandy 29

101st Airborne Division (Screaming Eagles) 15, 17, 29–30, 77

173rd Airborne Brigade 117–209; awards and decorations 211; Combat Service Identification Badge *117*; constant movement around South Vietnam 165–166; Dak To battles 111; Dorn's transfer to 111–112, 114; Headquarters 115, 118, 174; Property Book Officer 114–115; *see also* 1st Battalion, 503rd PIR; Reconnaissance Platoon, E Company

Operation Market-Garden 16

Operation Ranch Hand 28

pacification 176–178, 182, 186–188

parachute flares 52–53

parachuting, Dorn's enjoyment of 2–3

Patton, George S. 77

PCS (Permanent Change of Station) status 23–24

peaches *vs.* bamboo viper 165

Pentagon: ambush bean counter 148–149, 159; RRU inquiry 25–26

Permanent Change of Station (PCS) status 23–24

phone calls 47–48, 52

Phu Bai village 15; *see also* Gia Le Combat Base

pineapple plantation reconnaissance 81–88

PIO *see* Public Information Officer

plasma transfusions 205–206

Playboy Club, Miami 171

Playboy Playmate 191

Pleiku Air Base 140, 165

Pope Air Force Base, North Carolina 5, 6, 8–9, 24

Post Exchange (PX) officer, Dorn as 35–46; Army Commendation Medal 48; beer and soda "liberation" 37–38, 46; budget 35; calling home 47–48; challenges 35–36; Da Nang Officer's Club 44–45; Da Nang PX Depot 35, 36–38; Da Nang restaurant 40–41; Da Nang rocket attack 41–43; Dorn's dizziness and unconsciousness 43–44; ice cream 38–40; near death experiences 41–44; redeployment to Saigon Capital Military District 47–48; storage unit 45

Powell, Colin 13

PRC-25 radio 119–120, 203, 205

Presidio, San Francisco 111–112

"Prior Planning Prevents Piss Poor Performance" 54

prisoners of war 27, 29, 195

Public Information Officer (PIO), Dorn as 17–34; Army Commendation Medal 48;

Index

Index

member as Kit Carson Scout 84–86, *85*; Hai Van Pass ambushes 36; LV Uplift area 177, 178–180; mapping trails and fortifications of 202; mudflats 94–95; pineapple plantation 81–84; RDU's waterboarding of 192–196; Reconnaissance Platoon's encounter with assistant finance chief and bodyguard 128–129; rocket launch system 63; Saigon "Rocket Belt" attacks 63; shadow Province Government 129; Tet Offensive 6, 13, 20, 54, 58, 59, 212

Vietnam: awards and decorations 21, 31, 211; Dorn's arrival 2, 12–13; Dorn's deployment orders 4–8; Dorn's transport to 8–11; humidity 6–7, 12, 32; monsoon season 7, 32; National Route 1A 35–36, 38

Vietnam Service Medal 211

Vietnamese Army 39–40

Vietnamese people, positive interactions with: boat ride to village 102–104; chit-chat 85; helping rebuild the village and a feast 186–188; MEDCAPS 21–22; mini–MEDCAPS 102–104, 178; pacification 176–178, 182, 186–188

Vinh family 39–41

viper *vs.* peaches 165

war crimes 192–196

War Zone D 114

waterboarding 192–196

Wayne, John 204

Westmoreland, William 6

white phosphorus grenades 109

white star clusters 52–53

Whitman, Stuart 204

World War I 3

World War II: Bastogne 16, 77; "Bouncing Betty" mines 167; D-Day 16, 17, 29, 96; Dorn family military service 8; 82nd Division 3; Paratroopers 16, 17; war crimes 196

York, Alvin 3